STEVE SPANGLER'S

MIND-BLOWING
SCIENCE
EXPERIMENTS

FOR KIDS AND
THEIR FAMILIES

SCIENCE

DISCOVERING HOW THE WORLD WORKS

If you've ever wanted to learn more about what makes certain things fly or float, why combining certain chemicals yields explosive results or how you can lie down on a bed of nails without hurting yourself, there's a scientific explanation for that! By performing all the experiments in this book, you and a group of friends can learn about the incredible forces and scientific principles that impact different aspects of our lives every day. Read on to discover how you can put science to the test!

SCIENCE SUPPLIES

WHILE MOST OF THESE EXPERIMENTS CAN BE CONDUCTED WITH COMMON HOUSEHOLD ITEMS, SOME REQUIRE MORE SPECIALIZED MATERIALS, SUCH AS ¼"-20 HEX NUTS, PVC, DISPOSABLE PIPETTES, ETC. THESE CAN BE FOUND AT YOUR LOCAL CRAFT SHOP, HARDWARE STORE OR ONLINE RETAILERS.

IT'S ELEMENTARY

COLLABORATION IS KEY

BEHIND EVERY GREAT SCIENTIST, THERE IS A TEAM. We tend to picture the world's celebrated scientific minds as lone geniuses toiling away in cave-like laboratories, bent reverently over tables strewn with bubbling beakers, scribbling observations by the light of Bunsen burners. That's not to say some textbook trailblazers didn't prefer the quiet of solitude—Albert Einstein and Sir Isaac Newton, for instance—but it's easy to forget that even loners build on the hard work of those who came before them. In a word, all science comes down to collaboration, because science doesn't happen in a vacuum (unless you're testing whether or not a falcon feather falls at the same rate as a hammer on the moon, that is).

From Marie and Pierre Curie to Orville and Wilbur Wright to the fab four who discovered the double helix structure of DNA (James Watson, Francis Crick, Maurice Wilkins and Rosalind Franklin), history shows us that teamwork makes the dream work. Whether you specialize in chemistry, physics or repairing bicycles, among other fields of study, science is a process that draws on the previous discoveries of other inquiring minds who enlisted help with formulating hypotheses, acquiring equipment, conducting experiments, drawing conclusions and—this is key—people who then put those hypotheses to the test. It's an endless quest for knowledge, but that's what makes it exciting, and that's where this book comes in.

All of these experiments are designed to be demonstrated by a team, putting you at the center of a collaborative effort to test scientific principles developed over many years of study. Put simply, this

book gives you access to centuries of research in a matter of minutes! Loaded with amazing science facts and trivia, these activities make for some seriously ambitious (and colorful!) science fair projects guaranteed to jumpstart your journey to understanding the forces at work in the universe.

Grab your friends or family and get ready to make some incredible discoveries from the comfort of your home!

—Steve Spangler

SCIENCE SAFETY

While learning about science is tons of fun, it should go without saying that there are a few things to keep in mind when you gear up to conduct an experiment. What makes these activities exciting—sharp objects, fire, eruptions and other cool stuff—are the same things that crank up the danger factor. That's why you need to set up your space (or "lab") with safety in mind before starting any experiment.

1. ALWAYS ASK AN ADULT

Before you begin any science experiment, get your parent or guardian's permission. Even if you aren't going to work with anything notably dangerous, it's always best to get their approval before you stock up on supplies. You absolutely need an adult's help and supervision if an experiment calls for using a sharp blade or drill, heating substances or lighting something on fire.

2. READ ALL INSTRUCTIONS

This is the only way to ensure that you have everything you need for the experiment, that you understand what will happen whether or not it goes according to plan and that you stay safe before, during and after the experiment.

3. WEAR PROTECTIVE CLOTHING IF NECESSARY

Be sure to wear safety glasses when working with anything that shatters, bubbles, pops or explodes. You should also wear heavy gloves when working with hot objects.

4. WASH YOUR HANDS AFTER YOU'RE DONE EXPERIMENTING...

You don't want anything lingering on your skin after you complete your research.

5. ...AND DON'T TOUCH YOUR MOUTH OR EYES.

This is always sound advice in terms of keeping yourself healthy, but you definitely DO NOT want to get anything like vinegar in your eyes!

6. NO EATING OR DRINKING IN THE LAB

Keep food and drink out of the area where you're conducting your experiment. Doing this ensures you won't accidentally ingest one of your materials. Save that snack for later.

DURING ANY EXPERIMENT, ALWAYS KEEP LONG HAIR TIED BACK AND WEAR CLOSED-TOE SHOES.

THE SCIENTIFIC
METHOD

The scientific method helps us to understand how things work. It is hands-down the best tool we have to determine what is true.

Although many of the experiments in this book demonstrate concepts scientists know well, by using the scientific method, you can turn these activities into opportunities to explore the forces at work in our world step-by-step!

STEP 1: ASK A QUESTION

To get started, determine a subject you want to learn more about. For example, if you do the Color Mixing Wheel experiment on pg. 66, you might find yourself wondering, "How would other colors, like orange, green or white, look if I colored them in, too?" Start taking notes about the things you would like to compare.

A CONSTANT IS A COMPONENT OF A SCIENTIFIC EXPERIMENT THAT IS ALWAYS THE SAME. A VARIABLE IS A COMPONENT OF A SCIENTIFIC EXPERIMENT THAT CHANGES.

STEP 2: GATHER INFORMATION AND OBSERVE

You'll see this word a lot: "observe." It's the simplest way to dive in and begin learning about something. To continue the example from before, start to mull those other colors from Step 1 over in your mind a bit, focusing on how you might compare their ability to blend to the colors you've used on the first color mixing wheel or consider whether or not it would change anything if you shaded them in lightly.

STEP 3: FORM A HYPOTHESIS

Now that you've spent some time considering the colors, it's time to make an educated guess about how different they will look on a second color mixing wheel compared to your first color mixing wheel. This is what scientists call a hypothesis. What do you think will happen and why?

STEP 4: LET'S EXPERIMENT

Get ready for one of the most exciting steps in your scientific journey: testing your hypothesis! Recreate your original experiment using your new materials by designing another color mixing wheel, but be sure to change only one thing—otherwise known as a **variable**—at a time. In this case, you're changing one of the colors on the outer ring. Record your findings.

STEP 5: ANALYZE YOUR RESULTS

What happened? Was it what you expected or did something else occur? It's OK if things did not line up with your hypothesis. The amazing thing about science is that you can always make a new hypothesis to test!

STEP 6: DRAW YOUR CONCLUSION

Once you have the results of your experiment, you can share them with everyone! Write down why you undertook the experiment and what happened. If you aren't sure why something did or did not work as you imagined, do some more research and keep experimenting! Remember: There's always something new to learn.

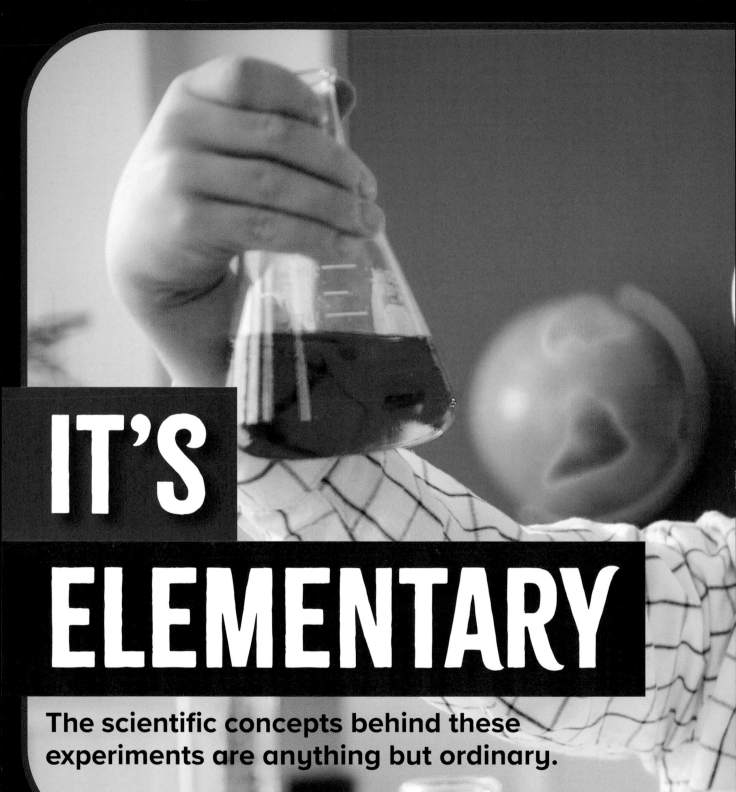

IT'S ELEMENTARY

The scientific concepts behind these experiments are anything but ordinary.

THE BALLOON KEBAB

SLIME GLACIER

ELEPHANT'S TOOTHPASTE

SLIME GLACIER

THE SCIENCE OF GLACIERS IN THE PALM OF YOUR HAND.

MATERIALS

2 8-Ounce Bottles of Elmer's Glue-All

BORAX
Borax

8-Ounce Plastic Cup

Spoon

Large Mixing Bowl

Water

Zipper-Lock Bag

Measuring Cup

Blue Food Coloring

Cookie Sheet or Plastic Tray

LET'S EXPERIMENT

1

TO MAKE the white batch of slime, empty one bottle of glue into a mixing bowl. Fill half the bottle with warm water, put the lid on and shake. Pour the glue-water mixture into the mixing bowl. Use the spoon to mix well.

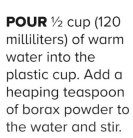

2

POUR ½ cup (120 milliliters) of warm water into the plastic cup. Add a heaping teaspoon of borax powder to the water and stir.

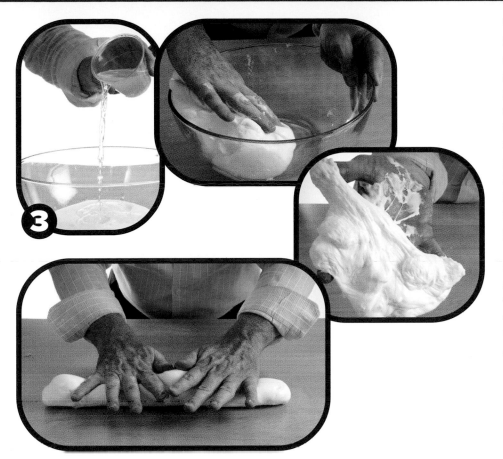

3

WHILE stirring the glue in the mixing bowl, slowly add a little of the borax solution. Immediately, you'll feel the long strands of molecules start to connect. At this point, use your hands to do the mixing. Keep adding the borax solution to the glue mixture (don't stop mixing) until the slime has a putty-like consistency.

You should be able to roll it on the table like dough, but if you let it rest for a couple of minutes, the slime will spread itself out. Set this batch of white slime off to the side.

REPEAT Steps 1–4 to make your blue batch of slime, but this time add about 10 drops of blue food coloring during Step 2. Try to keep the consistency of this batch the same as the previous batch.

4

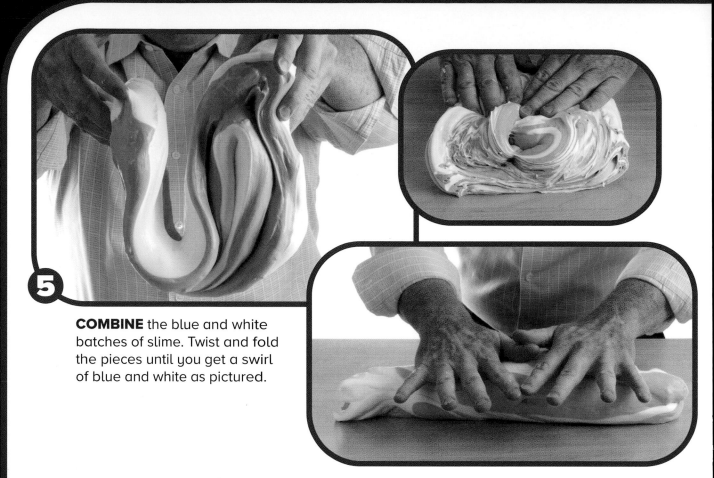

5

COMBINE the blue and white batches of slime. Twist and fold the pieces until you get a swirl of blue and white as pictured.

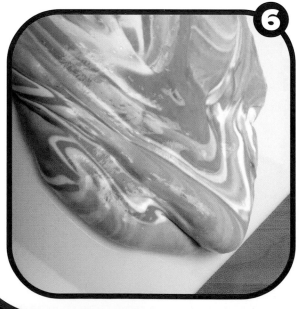

6

LAY the slime out on a cookie sheet or plastic tray. Use a few books to prop up one end. Place your slime on the sheet and allow it to slowly flow downhill. Observe how the blue and white slime creates some amazing patterns as the mixture flows downward.

At any point, you can pick up the slime, reshape it into a big blob, set it at the top of the cookie sheet and restart the flow. Try placing various sizes of rocks on the cookie sheet as obstacles for the slime to flow around. Depending on the size of the rock, the movement of the slime glacier might be powerful enough to push the rock down the hill.

Seal your slime in a zipper-lock bag for safekeeping.

HOW DOES IT WORK?

The mixture of Elmer's® Glue-All with borax and water produces a putty-like material called a **polymer**, or a long chain of molecules. If the long molecules slide past each other easily, then the substance acts like a **liquid** because the molecules flow. If the molecules stick together at a few places along the strand, then the substance behaves like a rubbery **solid** called an **elastomer**. Borax is the compound that is responsible for hooking the glue's molecules together to form the putty-like material.

The unique, slow-moving properties of the slime simulate the movement of a glacier. At a molecular level, ice is composed of stacked layers of molecules with relatively weak bonds between the layers, similar to the makeup of our slime molecules. Depending on how much **pressure** is applied, ice will either crack or break (which is what causes **crevasses** in glaciers), or, with low pressure, bend and stretch. The steady pressure from the bulk of the ice mass and the pull of gravity cause the glacier to flow slowly downhill.

TAKE IT FURTHER

ADJUST THE AMOUNTS of water, borax and glue to see how the consistency of the slime. Get the whole family together and create a slime race to see which slime moves the fastest—or the slowest—by placing them on a large cookie sheet and watching them move!

DID YOU KNOW?

FOR HUNDREDS OF THOUSANDS OF YEARS, THE MOVEMENT OF GLACIERS HAS SHAPED LAND THROUGH EROSION AND DEPOSITION, CREATING LANDFORMS SUCH AS U-SHAPED VALLEYS, MORAINES AND KETTLE LAKES, TO NAME A FEW.

FOLDING EGG

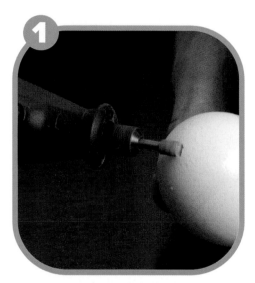

⚠️ **SAFETY NOTE**
Have an adult help you with this experiment!

🕐 **TIME NOTE**
This experiment takes up to 11 days to complete.

MATERIALS

Raw Eggs

Pin, Thumbtack, Sharp Knife, Dremel or Small Drill

Tall Glass or Jar

Toothpick

White Vinegar

Moist Towelette

LET'S EXPERIMENT

1

THIS step requires a little practice (and patience): You need to blow out the inside of the egg without causing too much visible damage. Have an adult use a pin, a thumbtack or the tip of a sharp knife to poke a small hole, about ⅛ inch in diameter, in both ends of the egg. (You can also use a Dremel or small drill.)

2

BREAK the yolk by inserting a toothpick (or a plastic coffee stirrer) through the hole. Carefully and gently poke around inside the egg to scramble it.

3

READ this step before you do it: While holding your egg over the sink or an empty glass, use the moist towelette to clean off one end of the egg, then cover the hole with your mouth and blow the liquid out of the other hole.

4

PLACE the hollow egg in a tall glass or jar and add enough vinegar to cover the egg. (You may need to place a large spoon on top of the egg to push it down, or try filling the inside of the egg with vinegar to weigh it down.)

LEAVE the egg in the vinegar for a full 24 hours.

5

THE NEXT day, pour out the vinegar and cover the egg with fresh vinegar. Set aside in a safe place for up to 10 days or until the shell has dissolved. For the first few days, bubbles of carbon dioxide (CO_2) will form on the shell.

ONCE the bubbles have stopped forming (up to 10 days), pour off the vinegar and carefully rinse the egg membrane with water.

CAREFULLY squeeze out all of the water from inside the egg membrane. When you gently blow air into one end of the egg, the egg will puff up. Slowly squeeze the egg in your hand and it will look like you crushed the egg. Carefully toss and bounce the "folded egg" in your hands to magically restore its shape.

6

HOW DOES IT WORK?

The acetic acid in the vinegar breaks down the calcium carbonate in the eggshell, and the bubbles that form on the surface of the egg are CO_2. Eventually, the hard shell of the egg disappears entirely and all that remains is the egg **membrane**. Because you have already blown out the contents of the egg, the membrane is just full of air. You can fold it up and the air will leak out of the tiny holes in the membrane that you used to blow the yolk out of the egg. The membrane will compress down into practically nothing. As you gently toss and bounce the "folded egg" on your hand, the air reenters the membrane, expanding it back into its original shape and volume.

TAKE IT FURTHER

FOR A MORE realistic-looking folding egg, dust the egg membrane with baby powder before it dries completely. Try to get some of the powder inside the egg as well. The powder helps keep the egg membrane from drying out and cracking, completing the look.

DID YOU KNOW?

AN EGG'S COLOR DEPENDS ON THE BREED OF THE HEN THAT LAID IT. WHITE LEGHORN HENS, FOR EXAMPLE, LAY WHITE EGGS, WHEREAS PLYMOUTH ROCKS AND RHODE ISLAND REDS LAY BROWN EGGS. OTHER NATURALLY-OCCURRING EGG COLORS INCLUDE BLUE-GREEN AND LIGHT PINK.

SINKING SODA SURPRISE

MATERIALS

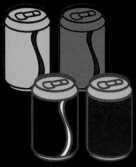

Unopened 12-Ounce Soda Cans: Diet, Regular, Brand Name, Generic (mini-cans will not work)

A 5-Gallon Bucket of Water (or an Aquarium)

LET'S EXPERIMENT

1

GRAB a can of regular soda and ask yourself: Will this can float? Place the can of regular soda in the water and observe. It sinks to the bottom.

GRAB a can of diet soda and ask yourself: Will this can float? Place the can of diet soda in the water and observe. It floats! Wobble the can from side to side to check that there are no bubbles trapped under the bottom. So why does it float?

2

3

EXPERIMENT with the various soda cans. Why do the regular sodas sink and the diet sodas float, no matter the brand?

TAKE IT FURTHER

REPEAT the experiment, only this time, use salt water instead of regular water. Are your results any different? What if you continue adding salt? How much salt do you have to add before your results change? Consider changing the temperature of the water or the temperature of the cans. Do either of those changes affect the results?

DID YOU KNOW?

A PACKET OF SUGAR CONTAINS ABOUT 4 GRAMS OF SUGAR, OR 15 CALORIES. THIS MEANS THAT THERE ARE ABOUT 10 PACKETS OF SUGAR IN A CAN OF REGULAR SODA, ACCOUNTING FOR THE 150 CALORIES. THAT'S A LOT OF SUGAR!

HOW DOES IT WORK?

You can determine how dense an object is by using the density equation: Density = Mass ÷ Volume. The density of water is 1.0 grams (g) per milliliter (mL). Any object that has a density greater than 1.0 g/mL will sink and any object with a density of less than 1.0 g/mL will float.

Volume refers to how much space an object occupies. For fluids, volume is usually measured in liters (L) or milliliters (mL). All the soda cans contain the same amount of liquid (355 mL), which means the only variable left to consider in the density equation is the mass.

If a diet and a regular soda can are placed on a double-pan balance scale, it quickly becomes clear that the regular soda is heavier (or has more mass) than the diet soda. Mass refers to how much stuff exists within an object, and for the purposes of our experiment, mass is measured in grams.

What's inside the can of regular soda that makes it so much heavier than diet soda? Comparing the list of ingredients on both cans, you see that a can of regular soda has about 150 calories while diet soda has 0 calories. All of those calories come from one place: sugar! Diet sodas usually contain aspartame, an artificial sweetener, while regular sodas use sugar. Take a look at the nutritional information on the side of the cans and see how much sugar is in a regular soda (under carbohydrates). Most regular sodas have between 39 and 43 grams of sugar. This added mass is why the cans of regular soda sink in water. By contrast, the relatively tiny amount of artificial sweetener used in diet soda has a negligible effect on the mass, enabling the can to float.

THE BABY DIAPER SECRET

YOU'LL NEVER LOOK AT DIAPERS THE SAME WAY AGAIN!

MATERIALS

Disposable Diapers (Several Brands)

8-Ounce Plastic Cup

Zipper-Lock Bag

Scissors

Construction Paper (or Newspaper)

Water

LET'S EXPERIMENT

PLACE a diaper on top of a piece of construction paper. Using scissors, carefully cut through the inside lining of the diaper and remove all of the cotton-like material. Place all the stuffing into a clean zipper-lock bag.

1

SCOOP up any of the polymer powder that may have spilled onto the construction paper and pour it into the bag with the stuffing. Blow just enough air into the bag to make it puff up like a pillow, then seal the bag.

2

3

SHAKE the bag for a few minutes to remove the powdery polymer from the stuffing. Notice the small amount of powder that falls to the bottom of the bag. You'll be amazed by what it can do!

CAREFULLY remove the stuffing from the bag.

4

POUR the polymer into a plastic cup and fill the cup with about 4 ounces (120 milliliters) of water. Mix it with your finger (or a spoon) until the mixture begins to thicken.

5

OBSERVE the gel that the polymer and water create. Turn the cup upside down and see how it has solidified. Neat!

HOW DOES IT WORK?

The secret, water-absorbing chemical in a diaper is a superabsorbent polymer called sodium polyacrylate. A polymer is a long chain of repeating molecules (these molecules are made of many smaller units, called **monomers**, which are joined together). Some polymers are made up of millions of monomers. Superabsorbent polymers expand tremendously when they come in contact with water because water is drawn into and held by the molecules of the polymer. Polymers act like giant sponges—some can soak up as much as 800 times their weight in water.

The cotton-like fibers you removed from the diaper help to spread out both the polymer and any other waste so that the baby wearing it doesn't have to sit on a mushy lump of water-filled gel. In spite of their usefulness, these diapers can be a problem. If you've ever observed a baby in diapers splashing in a wading pool, you know that even one diaper can absorb lots and lots of water. Most public pools won't allow them to be worn in the water because huge globs of gooey gel can leak out and make a mess of the filter system.

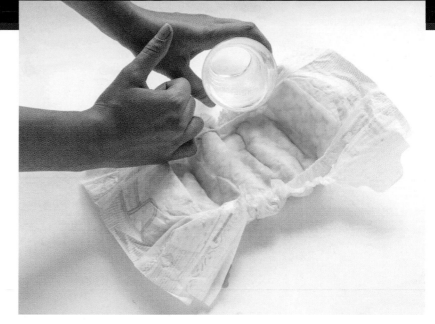

TAKE IT FURTHER

PUT THE PIECES of gel back into the cup and smush them down with your fingers. Add a teaspoon of salt, stir it with a spoon and watch what happens: Salt messes with the gel's water-holding abilities. When you're finished, pour the salt and water goo down the drain, grab a new diaper and slowly pour about ¼ cup of warm tap water into the center. Hold the diaper over a large pan or the sink and continue to add water, a little at a time, until it will hold no more. Keep track of how much water the diaper can absorb before it reaches its limit.

DID YOU KNOW?

SUPERABSORBENT POLYMERS ARE ALSO WIDELY USED IN SUCH APPLICATIONS AS FORESTRY, GARDENING AND LANDSCAPING AS A MEANS OF CONSERVING WATER.

BOUNCING BOO BUBBLES

⚠️

WARNING!
Never trap dry ice in a jar without a jar. There MUST be a hole in the jar to allow the pressure to escape or the pressure will build up and the jar will explode and cause serious harm to you or someone else!

NOTE: **Thick leather gloves are required for handling dry ice. Knit gloves do not provide enough protection for your hands.**

MATERIALS

 Safety Glasses

Gallon-Sized Plastic Jar

Thick Leather Gloves

3-Foot Piece of Rubber Tubing

 Liquid Soap (Dawn Works Best)

 Dry Ice

 Small Plastic Container

 Bath Towel

 Hammer

LET'S EXPERIMENT

TO MAKE your own Dry Ice Bubble Generator, you'll need a gallon-sized plastic jar with a 3-foot piece of rubber tubing attached to the side. The goal is to attach the tubing to the top part of the jar so that the fog created by mixing dry ice and water blows out of the tube when you cover the top of the jar with the lid. The free end of the rubber tubing is attached to a small funnel or something similar to help blow bubbles when it's dipped into a soapy water solution. To attach a piece of plastic tubing to the jar, you can drill a hole in the jar and attach the hose with a piece of tape or a dab of caulking or glue. The design is up to you.

1

WHILE wearing your safety glasses and thick leather gloves, use a hammer to break up the dry ice into pieces that will easily fit into the jar.

FILL half of the jar with warm water. Attach the rubber hose to the side of the jar (if it's not already attached).

DROP a few good-sized pieces of dry ice into the jar. Immediately, the fog will roll out of the jar. Practice covering the top of the jar with the lid to control the flow of fog out of the tube. Don't screw the lid onto the jar—just hold it on top to force more or less fog through the rubber tubing.

MIX a dash of liquid soap with about 4 ounces of water in the small plastic container.

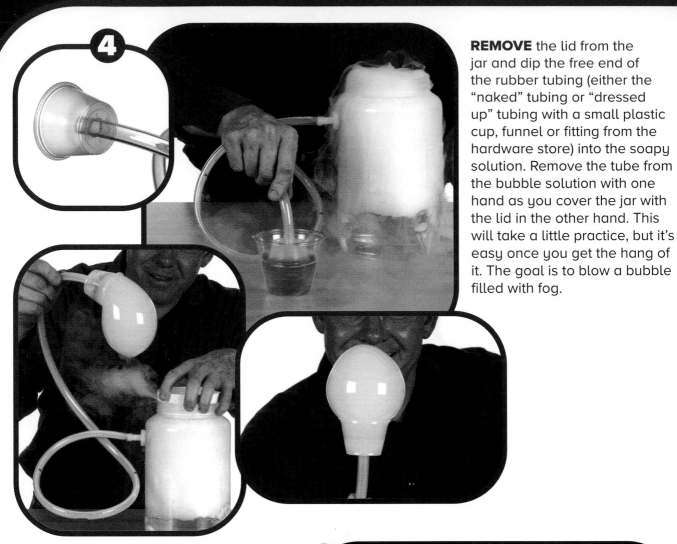

REMOVE the lid from the jar and dip the free end of the rubber tubing (either the "naked" tubing or "dressed up" tubing with a small plastic cup, funnel or fitting from the hardware store) into the soapy solution. Remove the tube from the bubble solution with one hand as you cover the jar with the lid in the other hand. This will take a little practice, but it's easy once you get the hang of it. The goal is to blow a bubble filled with fog.

WHEN the bubble reaches the perfect size, gently shake it off of the tubing and it will quickly fall to the ground (it's heavier than a normal bubble because it's filled with carbon dioxide gas and water vapor). When the bubble hits the ground, it bursts, and the cloud of fog erupts from the bubble. Very cool!

HOW DOES IT WORK?

Regular bubbles burst when they come in contact with just about anything because a bubble's worst enemies are oil and dirt. Soap bubbles will bounce off of a surface that's free of the oil or dirt particles that would normally puncture the soap film. They break when they hit the ground, but they don't break if they land on a softer fabric like gloves or a towel.

Dry ice is frozen carbon dioxide (CO_2). Under normal atmospheric conditions, CO_2 is a **gas**. Dry ice does not melt like real ice because it skips the liquid stage and goes straight from a solid to a gas—a process called sublimation. According to experts, dry ice will sublimate at a rate of 5 to 10 pounds every 24 hours in a typical vented ice chest. It's best to purchase the dry ice as close to the time you need it as possible because the dry ice in the grocery bag will vanish in about a day!

Grocery stores use dry ice to keep food cold during shipping. Some grocery stores and ice cream shops will sell dry ice to the public (especially around Halloween) for between $1 to $3 per pound. Dry ice comes in flat square slabs a few inches thick or as cylinders that are about 3 inches long and about half an inch in diameter. Either size will work fine for your dry ice experiments.

TAKE IT FURTHER

TOUCHABLE BOO BUBBLES!

If fog-filled bubbles will bounce off of a towel, what would happen if you wrapped your hands in fabric and tried to touch or play with the bubbles? Using winter gloves, blow a bubble about the size of a baseball with the Dry Ice Bubble Generator, then bounce the bubble off of your gloves. Also try bouncing it off of your shirt or pants (some fabrics work better than others), on a hand towel or start up a game of volleyball bubbles with another friend or two.

DID YOU KNOW?

ONLY ABOUT **0.035** PERCENT OF OUR ATMOSPHERE IS MADE UP OF CARBON DIOXIDE. MOST OF THE AIR WE BREATHE IS NITROGEN (79 PERCENT) AND OXYGEN (20 PERCENT).

ELEPHANT'S TOOTHPASTE

⚠️ **SAFETY NOTE**

Do not touch the foam with your bare hands! This could lead to burns.

MATERIALS

 1-Liter Plastic Soda Bottle

 Funnel

 Measuring Spoons

 Hydrogen Peroxide (12%, aka 40-Volume)

 Package of Dry Yeast

 Markers

 Small Plastic Container

 Liquid Dish Soap

 Rubber Gloves

 Plastic Tarp (To Cover the Table)

 **Construction Paper**

 Safety Glasses

 Food Coloring

LET'S EXPERIMENT

1

OPTIONAL: Using the construction paper and markers, make a decorative wrap that looks like a tube of toothpaste to cover the plastic soda bottle.

PUT on your safety glasses and remember to avoid touching the foam "toothpaste!" Rubber gloves provide an additional layer of protection if you have them handy.

2

COVER the demonstration table with the plastic tarp.

USE a funnel to add 4 ounces (120 mL) of 40-volume hydrogen peroxide to the 1-liter soda bottle.

ADD a squirt of dish soap and some food coloring to the hydrogen peroxide in the bottle. Give the solution a quick stir to mix the contents.

HAVE an adult help you with this step to prevent you from accidentally tipping over the bottle: Carefully cover the bottle with the toothpaste wrap.

MIX an entire package of dry yeast with 4 tablespoons of very warm water in a small plastic cup.

Stir the mixture with a spoon. If the mixture is too thick or paste-like, add a small amount of warm water to thin it out.

ONLY do this when you're ready: Pour the yeast mixture into the bottle and watch what happens. It may take a few seconds to react, but the result is well worth the wait! Observe.

When you are finished, it is safe to dispose of all of the materials either by throwing them in the trash can or by washing them down the drain.

HOW DOES IT WORK?

Hydrogen peroxide (H_2O_2) is made up of two hydrogen atoms and two oxygen atoms. H_2O_2 looks like ordinary water (H_2O), but the addition of that extra oxygen atom turns the molecule into an extremely powerful oxidizer. The yeast works as a **catalyst** to release the oxygen molecules from the hydrogen peroxide solution, while the oxygen-filled bubbles, which make up the foam, are actually the remainder of what happens when the hydrogen peroxide breaks down into water (H_2O) and oxygen (O_2). The bottle will feel warm to the touch because this is an **exothermic reaction** in which energy is given off in the form of heat.

DID YOU KNOW?

HYDROGEN PEROXIDE WAS USED AS THE MAIN FUEL SOURCE IN THE BELL ROCKET BELT, A JET PACK DESIGNED BY BELL AEROSYSTEMS IN THE LATE 1950S. THE SECOND ONE EVER BUILT CAN BE SEEN AT THE SMITHSONIAN NATIONAL AIR AND SPACE MUSEUM.

TAKE IT FURTHER

IF YOU REALLY WANT TO SEE HOW powerful exothermic reactions can be, check out the jumbo-sized version of this experiment on pg. 52, where sodium iodide crystals are the catalyst rather than yeast.

POP BOTTLE MUSIC

LET'S EXPERIMENT

MATERIALS

8 Identical Glass Bottles

Water

Spoon

FILL one bottle full with water and leave a second bottle empty. Use the back of the spoon to gently tap (or clink) both bottles. How are the sounds different?

FILL a third bottle half full with water. Using a spoon, clink all three bottles. The sound of the half-full bottle is somewhere in the middle of the other two sounds.

1

2

BLOW air across the tops of each bottle. What do you notice about the pitch of each bottle?

HOW DOES IT WORK?

The science of sound is all about vibrations. When you hit the bottle with the spoon, the glass vibrates, and it's these vibrations that ultimately make the sound. You discovered that tapping an empty bottle produced a higher-pitched sound than tapping a bottle full of water did. Adding water to the bottle dampens the vibrations created by striking the glass with a spoon. The less water in the bottle, the faster the glass vibrates and the higher the pitch. The more water you add to the bottle, the slower the glass vibrates, creating a lower pitch.

The same bottle that makes a low-pitched sound when you tap it with a spoon makes a high-pitched sound when you blow across the top. The same bottle produces opposite sounds! When you blow into the bottle, you are making the air vibrate, not the glass. An empty bottle produces a lower pitch because there's lots of air in the bottle to vibrate. Adding water to the bottle decreases the amount of air space, which means there is less air to vibrate. With less air, the vibrations happen more quickly and produce a higher pitch.

TAKE IT FURTHER

BY VARYING THE AMOUNTS OF WATER IN EACH BOTTLE, it's possible to create a musical scale (that's why this experiment calls for eight bottles, one for each note of the musical scale). Try clinking the bottles and blowing over the tops of the bottles. What differences do you notice? You can also use food coloring to color the water in each bottle differently and try to play a song. Of course, the food coloring does nothing to affect the sound, but it does make it look like you really know what you're doing!

Invite some friends over and present them with this challenge: In 60 seconds, arrange the bottles in such a way that when they are clinked with the spoon, they play a familiar song. Try "Jingle Bells," "Mary Had a Little Lamb," "Twinkle, Twinkle Little Star" or even Beethoven's Fifth Symphony—the song is up to you. The first person to arrange the bottles correctly and play the song wins!

DID YOU KNOW?

THIS EXPERIMENT IS ESSENTIALLY RECREATING A GLASS HARP (ALSO KNOWN AS MUSICAL GLASSES OR SINGING GLASSES), A MUSICAL INSTRUMENT COMPOSED OF A GROUP OF WINE GLASSES FILLED WITH VARIOUS AMOUNTS OF WATER THAT FIRST BECAME POPULAR IN THE MID-18TH CENTURY.

THE BALLOON KEBAB

LET'S EXPERIMENT

INFLATE the balloon until it's nearly full, then let about a third of the air out. Tie a knot in the end of the balloon.

If you carefully examine the balloon, you'll notice a thick area of rubber at both the top and bottom (where you tied the knot and at the opposite end). This is where you will pierce the balloon with the skewer (don't do it yet!).

MATERIALS

Several Latex Balloons (9-Inch Size Works Well)

10-Inch Bamboo Cooking Skewers

Cooking Oil or Dish Soap

Sharpie Pen

1

COAT the wooden skewer with a few drops of vegetable oil or dish soap. Be careful not to point the skewer at anyone.

2 **READ** through these next two steps before you do them: Place the sharpened tip of the skewer on the thick end of the balloon and push the skewer into the balloon. Be careful not to jab yourself or the balloon with the skewer. Just use gentle pressure (and maybe a slight twisting motion) to puncture the balloon.

PUSH the skewer all the way through the balloon until the tip of the skewer touches the opposite end, where you'll find the other thick portion of the balloon. Keep pushing until the skewer penetrates the rubber. Success!

3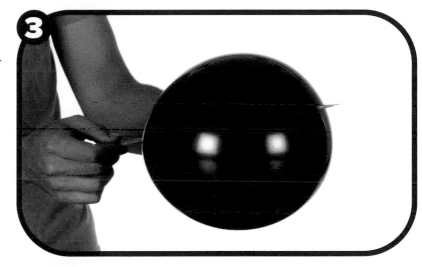

4 **GENTLY** remove the skewer from the balloon. The air will leak out of the balloon, but the balloon won't pop.

Repeat the experiment, but this time you'll see the hidden "stress" in your balloon.

1

BEFORE blowing up the balloon, use the Sharpie pen to draw about seven to ten dime-sized dots at both ends and in the middle of the balloon.

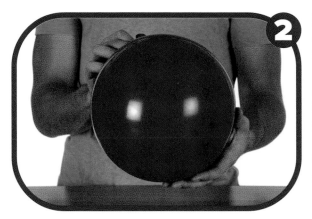

2

INFLATE the balloon halfway and tie the end. Observe the various sizes of the dots all over the balloon.

JUDGING from the size of the dots, where on the balloon are the latex molecules stretched out the most? Where are they stretched out the least?

COAT the skewer with a few drops of oil or dish soap.

USE the observations that you made previously about the dots on the balloon to decide the best spot to puncture the balloon with the skewer. Of course, the object is to **NOT** pop the balloon!

3

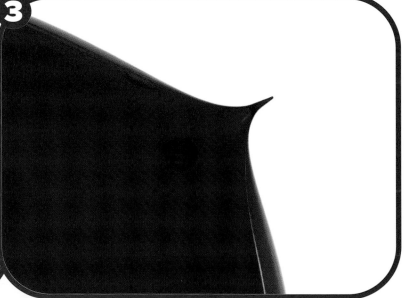

HOW DOES IT WORK?

On a microscopic level, the rubber that makes up the balloon is made of many long strands or chains of molecules called polymers, and the elasticity of these polymer chains causes rubber to stretch. Blowing up the balloon stretches these strands of polymer chains.

After drawing on the balloon with the Sharpie, you probably noticed that the dots on either end of the balloon were relatively small in comparison to the enlarged dots in the middle section of the balloon. That's because the ends of the balloon are known as the area of least stress. By piercing the balloon at a point where the polymer molecules were stretched out the least, the long strands of molecules stretched around the skewer and kept the air inside the balloon from rushing out. When you removed the skewer, you felt the air leaking out through the holes where the polymer strands were pushed apart. Eventually the balloon deflated, but it never popped.

TAKE IT FURTHER

BLOW UP A NEW BALLOON AND PLACE a small piece of clear tape in the middle of the balloon. Position the sharpened point of the skewer in the middle of the tape and carefully push the end of the skewer into the balloon without popping it! Try it again, but this time use a straight pin or the sharp end of a safety pin. What role does the tape play in keeping the balloon from popping?

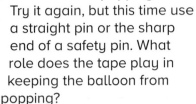

DID YOU KNOW?

WHILE MODERN BALLOONS ARE MADE FROM RUBBER OR LATEX, THE AZTECS CREATED BALLOONS FROM ANIMAL INTESTINES AND BLADDERS.

COAT HANGER TUNING FORK

MATERIALS

48-Inch (122-cm) String

Metal Hanger

Silverware

Table (Or Other Hard Surface)

THIS EXPERIMENT IS ALL ABOUT GOOD VIBRATIONS.

LET'S EXPERIMENT

CUT the piece of string into two pieces of equal length. Attach a piece of string to each end of the coat hanger.

NEXT, take the loose ends of each string and wrap three or four loops around the first knuckle on each index finger.

COVER the opening of each of your ears with a string-wrapped fingertip. Do not push your fingertips into your ears.

YOU'LL need to bend over a little so the hanger is dangling freely below you. You might need to do some more wraps around one or both fingers to keep the strings tight. Be sure your fingers completely cover your ear openings.

STANDING near a table, slightly rock your body forward and back to start the hanger swinging away from you, then toward you. Make sure the strings do not touch your cheeks when you're doing this. You want the hanger to tap the edge of the table lightly and bounce off, and you may need to back away from the table after a tap. What do you hear?

TAKE your fingers away from your ears and tap the hanger against the table again. There's quite a difference between clink-clink and bong!

TAP the hanger against different surfaces. Even soft surfaces will make the hanger vibrate. Listen carefully until the sounds fade away and then do it again. Try tapping different places on the hanger against the same surface. You'll find that the longer the section of hanger you tap, the more likely you are to get longer-lasting sounds.

HOW DOES IT WORK?

You've undoubtedly heard the sound metal coat hangers make when they bump up against each other in the closet. The noise that you hear is produced because the metal in the coat hanger is vibrating. The string you attached to the coat hanger carries the vibrations directly to your ears (through your fingertips). Tapping the hanger on an object makes the metal vibrate. The string then vibrates, and your ears detect the unusual sounds.

TAKE IT FURTHER
ATTACH A THICKER OR THINNER PIECE OF string to an identical coat hanger and observe the difference. Test out other coat hangers made out of different materials to see which ones make the coolest sounds. In place of a coat hanger, try attaching a spoon or fork to a piece of string to see what kinds of strange noises it can produce.

DID YOU KNOW?

THE SCIENCE OF SOUND IS CALLED ACOUSTICS, FROM THE GREEK AKOUSTOS, OR "HEARD." PHILOSOPHERS LIKE PYTHAGORAS AND ARISTOTLE WROTE ABOUT THE NATURE OF SOUND, BUT GALILEO GALILEI IS CREDITED AS THE FIRST BRIGHT MIND TO CONDUCT MODERN SCIENTIFIC EXPERIMENTS ON FREQUENCY AND PITCH.

MAGICAL MILK OF MAGNESIA

⚠ SAFETY NOTE
Have an adult help you with this experiment!

MATERIALS

Milk of Magnesia (Available at the Pharmacy)

White Vinegar

Red Cabbage

Large Glass or Cylinder

Strainer

Pitcher

Mixing Spoon

LET'S EXPERIMENT

1 **TO MAKE** a chemical "indicator"—a solution that will change color depending on the pH (see p. 51) of the liquid—remove 3 or 4 leaves of red cabbage and place them in a blender filled with water.

2 **BLEND** the leaves into very tiny pieces until the water turns purple.

3 **USE** a strainer to filter out all of the small pieces of red cabbage. You should be left with a pitcher of purple liquid (with the lovely smell of cabbage).

FILL the large glass or cylinder three-quarters full with cabbage juice.

ADD 1 to 2 ounces of milk of magnesia to the cabbage juice (the amount does not have to be exact). The chemical name for milk of magnesia is magnesium hydroxide—$Mg(OH)_2$.

The cabbage juice will turn light blue, indicating that it is slightly "basic" (that's the opposite of "acidic") because milk of magnesia is slightly basic.

WHILE stirring the solution with a large spoon, add a few ounces of white vinegar. The bluish liquid will quickly turn red!

CABBAGE juice turns bright red in the presence of an acid like vinegar, but... why does it gradually turn back to blue?

ADD more vinegar and watch as the liquid changes from blue to red, maybe a little yellow to green and back to bluish-purple.

EVENTUALLY, all of the vinegar (acid) will react with the magnesium hydroxide and the solution will remain purple.

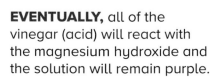

HOW DOES IT WORK?

Scientists measure acids and bases according to the pH scale. Acids have a low pH (0–6) and bases have a high pH (8–14), while neutral substances, like water, have a pH of 7. To determine if a substance is an acid or a base, scientists use an indicator, which is typically a chemical that changes color if it comes in contact with an acid or a base. Red cabbage contains a water-**soluble** pigment called anthocyanin that changes color when it is mixed with an acid or a base.

The chemical name for milk of magnesia is magnesium hydroxide ($Mg(OH)_2$). As an antacid, the hydroxide ions from the milk of magnesia combine with acid H+ ions in the stomach to neutralize the liquids there. The reason the purple cabbage juice changed to a bluish color when you added the milk of magnesia is because the solution turned slightly basic with the addition of the hydroxide ion. When you added vinegar to the mixture of cabbage juice and milk of magnesia, the solution turned red, indicating the presence of the acid H+ ions.

DID YOU KNOW?

ANTACIDS LIKE **MILK OF MAGNESIA CAN HELP NEUTRALIZE OUR STOMACHS WHEN WE'VE OVERINDULGED IN FOODS SUCH AS PIZZA, PROCESSED SNACKS, FRIED FOOD, CHEESE, CHOCOLATE, COFFEE, TOMATO-BASED SAUCES, BACON, CITRUS FRUITS AND MORE. ONE SIMPLE WAY TO FIGHT HEARTBURN: EAT A MORE BALANCED DIET!**

ELEPHANT'S TOOTHPASTE (THE JUMBO-SIZED VERSION)

TAKE THE EXPERIMENT FROM PG. 36 TO THE NEXT LEVEL!

⚠️ **SAFETY NOTE**

Have an adult help you with this experiment!

MATERIALS

Sodium Iodide Crystals (A Dry Chemical That Looks Like Salt)

Hydrogen Peroxide (30%)

Rubber Gloves

250-mL Beaker

Dish Soap

Measuring Spoons

Safety Glasses

Spoon

Food Coloring

Table

Graduated Cylinder

Plastic Tarp (To Cover the Table)

LET'S EXPERIMENT

1

2

3

COVER the table with the plastic tarp.

WEARING your safety glasses and rubber gloves, fill a beaker with 4 ounces (120 mL) of room temperature water. Add about 1 tablespoon of sodium iodide crystals and stir with a spoon until all of the crystals dissolve. Repeat this several times until the crystals no longer dissolve in the water and you have what is called a saturated solution. Label the beaker "Sodium Iodide Catalyst" and set it aside.

MEASURE 2 ounces (60 mL) of the 30% hydrogen peroxide into the graduated cylinder. Position the graduated cylinder in the middle of the plastic tarp.

ADD a squirt (about 5 mL) of dish soap to the graduated cylinder containing the 30% hydrogen peroxide.

ADD a few generous drops of your favorite food coloring. Stir the solution to mix the contents.

READ this step before you do it: pour 1 tablespoon (about 5 mL) of the sodium iodide catalyst into the graduated cylinder and quickly stand back. Within seconds, the reaction will occur and a mountain of erupting foam will cover the table.

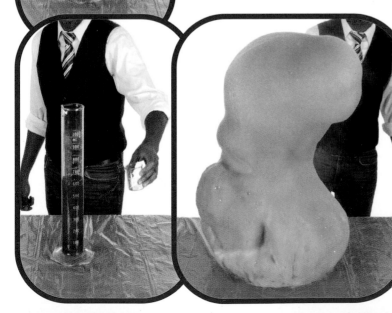

HOW DOES IT WORK?

For more info on how this experiment works, turn to pg. 39!

TAKE IT FURTHER

TRY PERFORMING THIS experiment inside your jack-o'-lantern! Instead of using a graduated cylinder, simply use a glass beaker to hold the 2 ounces of hydrogen peroxide along with the squirt of dish soap and the food coloring. With your safety glasses on, place the beaker inside a carved pumpkin. Add 1 tablespoon of saturated sodium iodide solution, then immediately replace the lid of the jack-o'-lantern and...success!

DID YOU KNOW?

FRENCH CHEMIST **LOUIS JACQUES THENARD DISCOVERED HYDROGEN PEROXIDE IN 1818.**

FUN WITH
PHYSICS

Discover the science behind light waves, sound waves, lift, friction and more!

UNBELIEVABLE FLOATIES

COLOR MIXING WHEEL

SKATEBOARD ROCKET CAR

MAGNETIC MONEY

LET'S EXPERIMENT

U.S. currency is not magnetic—it's not possible to pick up coins using a magnet, and everyone knows that paper isn't magnetic, right? Get ready to have your mind blown!

SEE IF YOU CAN PICK UP ON WHAT MAKES BILLS MAGNETIC.

$1 Bill (U.S. Currency—A Fresh, Crisp Bill Works Best)

Neodymium Magnet (Look for One at the Hardware Store)

1 **FOLD** the dollar bill in half, widthwise.

2 **HOLD** the dollar bill by one end so that the loose end hangs in the air.

SLOWLY bring the neodymium magnet close to the loose, hanging end of the bill. When you get just a few centimeters away, the bill will jump to the magnet!

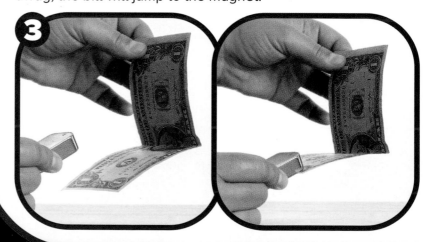

3

REPEAT this several times to confirm what you're observing. Switch ends of the bill to see if there is any difference. Try other denominations—$5, $10, $20, even $100.

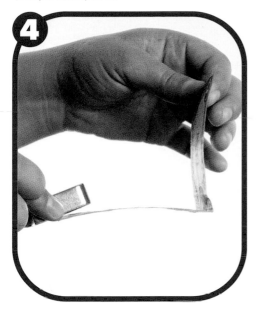

HOW DOES IT WORK?

The United States Treasury Department uses specially-made magnetic inks to print certain denominations of our money as a way to catch counterfeiters. While we don't know the exact make up of the magnetic ink, it's safe to assume there are tiny particles of iron or other magnetic metals like iron, nickel, cobalt and some alloys of rare earth metals, which is why the bill is attracted to the magnet.

IF YOU want to search for more of these tiny particles of iron and magnetic metals, go outside! Your house has probably been bombarded with hundreds if not thousands of micrometeorites. To find them, the next time it rains, place a bucket under a drain spout to collect a good amount of rain. Remove leaves and other big debris, then sift the remains through a bit of old window screen. Use the neodymium magnet and look closely to see if any of the remaining particles contain iron. Those particles may be space dust, also known as micrometeorites.

DID YOU KNOW

NEODYMIUM IS **A CHEMICAL ELEMENT WITH THE SYMBOL ND AND ATOMIC NUMBER 60. NEODYMIUM MAGNETS (ALSO KNOW AS RARE EARTH MAGNETS) ARE 10 TIMES STRONGER THAN STANDARD CERAMIC MAGNETS AND ARE COMMONLY USED IN SPEAKERS AND COMPUTER DISC DRIVES.**

FLYING POTATOES

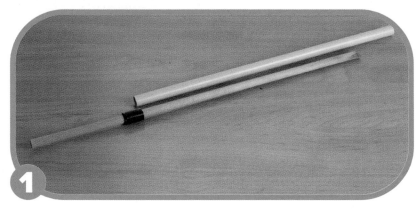

MATERIALS

Two 20-Inch Pieces of Dowel Rod
(With a 3/8-Inch Diameter)

16-Inch PVC Tube
(With a 1/2-Inch Diameter)

Duct Tape

Sack of Potatoes

Knife

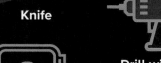

Drill with a Cone-Shaped Grinding Point (Optional)

Safety Glasses

LET'S EXPERIMENT

1

THERE are two parts to the potato launcher: the plunger (your dowel rod) and the PVC tube, both of which should be close to the same length. To create the plunger, form a stopper by wrapping a 12-inch strip of duct tape around one of the dowel rods approximately 6 inches from the end of the rod. (The photos show the best placement for the tape.) Do not wrap any tape around the second dowel rod.

2 **IN ORDER** for a piece of potato to fit tightly in the tube, it's necessary to flare both ends of the PVC tube. Have an adult help you use a knife to flare the edges. Use care, as the ends of the tube can be sharp or have rough edges. Or have an adult use an electric drill and a cone-shaping grinding point.

3

PLACE the potato on a flat surface. (If the potato is very thick, you might want to cut it in half lengthwise.) Hold the potato securely with one hand while carefully pushing the end of the tube through the potato with the other hand. Pull the tube out of the potato to see your "potato plug." (The sharpened, flared edges of the tube should help cut through the potato—but be very careful as the tube could cut your hands as well if it slips.)

HOLD the plunger (dowel rod) with your hand behind the stopper you made out of duct tape. Use the plunger to move the piece of potato to the other end of the tube (the tape stopper will position the potato plug a few inches from the other end). The photo of the clear PVC tubing in Step 5 shows the proper positioning of the potato plug. Always keep your pushing hand away from the sharp edge of the tube and firmly behind the tape stopper. Remove the plunger.

4

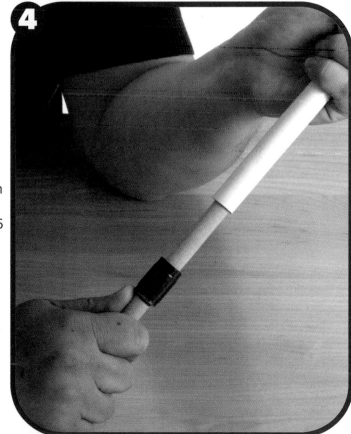

POSITION the potato securely on a flat surface while pushing the flared edges of the empty end of the tube into the potato again. Now both ends of the potato tube are plugged.

ASSUMING you're right-handed, hold the plastic tube in the middle with your left hand and the plunger in your right hand. The plunger will go into the end where the first potato plug is a few inches from the end of the tube.

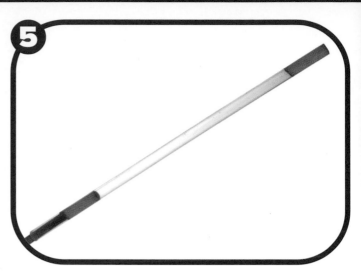

PUSH upward with the plunger on the bottom piece of potato until the top potato piece pops out of the tube. POW! The first piece of potato will shoot out at a high speed. Be sure not to aim the tube at anyone when you do this. Because of the placement of the duct tape stopper, the bottom potato should now be positioned a few inches from the top of the tube, and the bottom end of the tube is ready for another piece of potato.

WHEN you are finished, use the second dowel rod without the duct tape stopper to carefully push the remaining potato plug out of the tube, then wash and rinse the tube and the plunger with mild soap and water so you can use it again!

HOW DOES IT WORK?

The potato gun beautifully illustrates Boyle's Law, which states that pressure and volume are inversely proportional. In other words, as you decrease the volume of the air trapped in between the two pieces of potato, the pressure exerted by the air increases. This increase in pressure eventually forces the potato at the top end to exit the tube with a tremendous POP!

DID YOU KNOW?

IN THE U.S., POTATOES ARE GROWN IN ALL 50 STATES. IN 1995, THE HUMBLE SPUD BECAME THE FIRST VEGETABLE TO BE GROWN IN SPACE.

SCREAMING BALLOON

MATERIALS

Clear Latex Balloons (9-Inch Helium Balloons From a Party Store Work Best)

¼-Inch Hex Nuts

LET'S EXPERIMENT

INSERT a hex nut into the mouth of the balloon. Make sure the hex nut goes all the way to the bottom so there is no danger of it being sucked out while you blow up the balloon.

BLOW up the balloon, but be careful not to overinflate it, since it can easily burst!

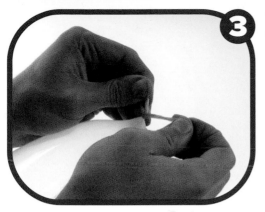

3 **TIE OFF** the end of the balloon.

WITH the palm of your hand touching the tied-off end of the balloon, gently but firmly grab the balloon, holding it palm-down.

4

BEGIN swirling the balloon in a circular motion. The hex nut may bounce around at first, but it will soon start to roll around the inside of the balloon. What is that "screaming" sound?

ONCE the hex nut begins to spin, use your other hand to stabilize the balloon. Your hex nut should continue to spin for 10 seconds or more,

HOW DOES IT WORK?

The primary **force** in action here is **centripetal (or center-seeking) force:** The inward force on a body that causes it to move in a circular path. In this case, it's the shape of the balloon that makes the hex nut move in a circular path. Otherwise, the hex nut would want to continue to move in a straight line. Another force to consider is **friction.** There's very little friction between the edge of the hex nut and the balloon. If there were more friction, it would cause the hex nut to slow down and stop.

A hex nut has six sides, and these flat edges cause the hex nut to bounce or vibrate inside the balloon. The screaming sound you hear is made by the sides of the hex nut vibrating against the inside wall of the balloon.

TAKE IT FURTHER

WHAT HAPPENS when you change the size of the balloon or the size of the hex nut? Or if you try two or three hex nuts? Try using a marble in place of a hex nut—does the marble make the balloon "scream"?

COLOR MIXING WHEEL

⚠️ **SAFETY NOTE**
Have an adult help you with this experiment!

MATERIALS

White Corrugated Cardboard

Pointed Lip Scissors

Ruler

Red, Blue and Yellow Markers

Pen

String or Yarn

Large Plastic Cup

Soda Bottle Cap

LET'S EXPERIMENT

To Create the Wheel...

USING the mouth of the plastic cup as a template, take a pen and trace a circle onto a piece of white corrugated cardboard. Try to get the circle to be between 4 to 6 inches in diameter.

USE the bottom of the plastic cup to trace a smaller-sized circle onto the cardboard disc. For the third circle, trace around a plastic soda bottle cap.

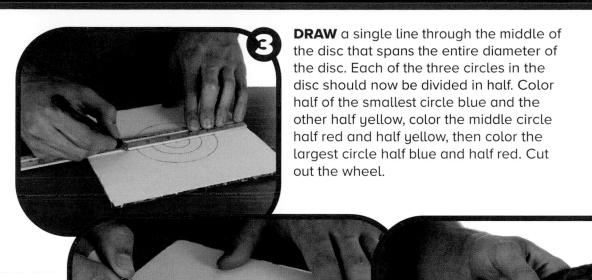

DRAW a single line through the middle of the disc that spans the entire diameter of the disc. Each of the three circles in the disc should now be divided in half. Color half of the smallest circle blue and the other half yellow, color the middle circle half red and half yellow, then color the largest circle half blue and half red. Cut out the wheel.

MEASURE and mark two holes in the cardboard disc, an equal distance from the center and about 1 inch apart. Use the pointed tip of the scissors to perforate the disc.

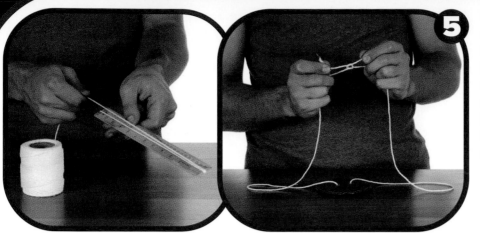

CUT a 4-foot-long piece of string or yarn, then thread it through each of the holes in the disc. Tie the ends of the string together in a knot as shown in the photograph. Make sure the knot is tight and can withstand a substantial amount of force.

To Do the Experiment...

HOLD the string on both sides of the disc as shown and slide the disc to as close to the center of the string as possible.

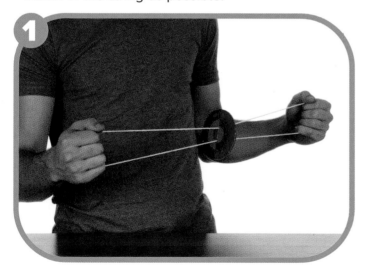

SPIN the disc in a motion similar to turning a jump rope to get the string wound up.

ONCE the string on both sides of the disc is twisted, pull the string tight to get the Color Mixing Wheel spinning (this might take a little practice).

WHEN you have the hang of how the Color Mixing Wheel works, you'll be able to keep it going as long as you want.

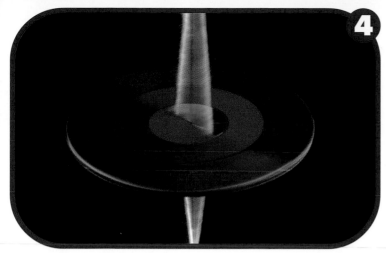

4 **YOU** may have noticed that the colors you put on the Color Mixing Wheel were the three primary colors: red, blue and yellow. Once you start spinning the wheel, what do you notice about each of the three colored circles on the cardboard disc? What do you think makes this happen?

HOW DOES IT WORK?

When you combine two primary colors, you create one of the secondary colors: purple, green or orange. The individual colors on the wheel appear to mix due to the speed at which the wheel is spinning as the string twists. The colors spin so quickly that your brain is unable to process them as the individual colors that you originally saw on the wheel. Instead, your brain takes a shortcut and creates the secondary colors.

Once you have the string twisted, pulling on each end makes it tight. When the string is pulled tight, it wants to be completely straight. To become straight, the string unwinds itself and causes the disc to spin in one direction. But the string doesn't stop once it's unwound—it speeds past and gets twisted again in the other direction. The momentum from pulling the string tight keeps the disc spinning until all the momentum is gone. Then you pull the strings tight again and set the disc spinning in another direction.

DID YOU KNOW?

YEARS AFTER **SIR ISAAC NEWTON AUTHORED HIS THEORIES ON THE LAWS OF MOTION, HE PENNED** *OPTICKS* **(1704), WHICH EXPLORED THE NATURE OF LIGHT. HE ALSO DESIGNED A REFLECTING TELESCOPE IN 1668.**

SKATEBOARD ROCKET CAR

MATERIALS

2-Liter Plastic Soda Bottle

Roll of Mentos Mints

Duct Tape

Skateboard

Safety Glasses

LET'S EXPERIMENT

1

PLACE a full 2-liter soda bottle on top of the skateboard so the soda will have a clear shot backward when it shoots out of the bottle. Before securing the bottle, check the design of the skateboard. If the skateboard tips curve up on the ends, the geyser might be deflected and the skateboard won't move much. You may need to add layers of cardboard to the top side of the skateboard (see photo for Step 2) so that when you tape the soda bottle to it, the rocket "exhaust" clears the curved tip.

WHEN you've got the bottle placed just right, have a friend or family member hold it tightly as you wrap duct tape once around the lower end of the bottle and the skateboard and once around the top end near its tip.

PUT the system on the ground and check the alignment of the bottle with the skateboard. It should be straight and centered, and the mouth of the bottle should be above the curved tips of the skateboard. Wrap two more layers of duct tape around each end of the system directly on top of the first layer.

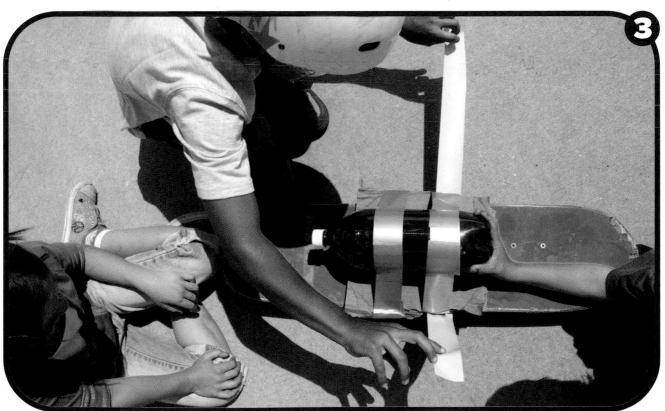

HOLD the system off of the ground, keeping it vertical, with the top of the bottle pointing up. Remove the bottle cap.

READ this next step before you do it: Ask an adult to open one end of the Mentos package and loosen the mints a little so they can slide out easily. You or the adult should hold the mints in one hand and place the open end of the Mentos package above the mouth of the bottle. Then, lift the package straight up and slide all of the Mentos mints into the soda all at once with the other hand. Do this by pinching the closed end of the wrapper between your fingers and sliding the mints toward the open end. This will push the Mentos quickly into the bottle in one continuous motion.

4

NOTE: It is essential to drop the mints into the bottle all at the same time.

There's only a split second to set the system on the ground before the geyser erupts and shoves the Skateboard Rocket Car downrange. Once the Mentos drop into the bottle, place the Skateboard Rocket Car on the ground fast and get out of the way! Success!

HOW DOES IT WORK?

What gives soda its bubbly appeal is invisible **carbon dioxide** gas (CO_2), which is forced into the liquid using tons of pressure. Until you open a soda, the gas mostly stays suspended in the liquid and can't collect to form bubbles. Aside from shaking the soda, there are other ways to cause the gas to escape: Just drop something into a glass of soda and notice how bubbles immediately form on the surface of the object.

Each Mentos mint has thousands of micro-pits, aka nucleation sites, all over its surface, and they're perfect places for CO_2 bubbles to form. As soon as the Mentos hit the soda, bubbles form all over the surfaces of the mints and then quickly rise to the surface of the liquid. The gas released by the Mentos pushes all of the liquid up and out of the bottle in an incredible soda blast. The geyser continues to erupt as long as the pits remain on the surface of the mints. Eventually, enough of the surface is dissolved so that it becomes too smooth for the gas to rapidly collect, and the reaction slows and stops.

According to **Newton's First Law Of Motion**, a Skateboard Rocket Car standing still will remain standing still and a moving Skateboard Rocket Car will continue moving in a straight line unless an outside force is strong enough to make the system move faster or slower, stop or change directions. **Newton's Second Law** says that to cause the system to move faster or slower, stop or change directions, the force used has to overcome the inertia (or motion) the Skateboard Rocket Car already has. **Newton's Third Law** states that for every action there is an equal and opposite reaction. The force of the soda geyser whooshing backward out the bottle is exactly matched by a force pushing the Skateboard Rocket Car forward. The stronger the backward geyser, the faster the car moves forward.

TAKE IT FURTHER

PERFORM THE activity again using a different variable—a different brand of diet soda, a different type of soda (regular instead of diet), a different sized bottle of soda, a different type of mint or a different skateboard—and record your results. What changed?

MASON JAR WATER SUSPENSION

MATERIALS

Pint-Size Mason Jar with Twist-On Lid

Plastic Screen Mesh (The Stuff Used to Make a Window Screen)

Scissors

Towels (For Spills)

Index Cards

LET'S EXPERIMENT

PLACE the plastic screen mesh over the opening of the jar and twist on the outside ring portion of the lid (the sealing band). Using scissors, cut around the lid to trim off the edges of the screen. If you want a more professional look, remove the lid before cutting the screen. The lid leaves an indentation in the screen material. Use scissors to cut around the indentation. What you're left with is a screen insert that fits perfectly into the top of the sealing band. Place the screen over the opening and twist on the band.

FILL the jar with water by simply pouring water through the screen.

COVER the opening with the index card. Hold the card in place as you turn the card and the jar upside down. Let go of the card. Surprisingly, the card remains attached to the lid of the upside-down jar.

CAREFULLY remove the card from the opening and the water mysteriously stays in the jar! Replace the card, turn the whole thing over, remove the card and try to pour out the water...amazing!

TAKE IT FURTHER

EXPERIMENT WITH different screens, some with fine mesh and some with coarse mesh, to observe how surface tension and air pressure work together to accomplish this feat (it's best to use plastic screen material since it will not rust or discolor the jar). Test out different kinds of plastic mesh (from produce bags, for example) to see how the size of the mesh affects the surface tension of the water.

HOW DOES IT WORK?

Atmospheric pressure (the pressure exerted by the surrounding air) is the force that holds the index card in place. The card stays on the upside-down jar because the pressure of the air molecules pushing up on the card is greater than the weight of the water pushing down. But how does the water stay in the jar when the card is removed? Simple: surface tension. The surface of a liquid behaves as if it has a thin membrane stretched over it. A force called cohesion, which is the attraction of similar molecules to each other, causes this effect. The water stays in the jar even though the card is removed because the molecules of water are joined together (through cohesion) to form a thin membrane between each tiny opening in the screen. Should you tip the jar, air will come into the jar, break the seal and cause the water to pour out. You can also break the surface tension by jiggling the jar or touching the screen. If you return the jar to its upright position, the air can no longer get into the jar and the rest of the water will stay inside.

DID YOU KNOW?

MASON JARS HAVE BEEN AROUND SINCE 1858 AND WERE INVENTED BY TINSMITH JOHN LANDIS MASON.

SELTZER POP ROCKET

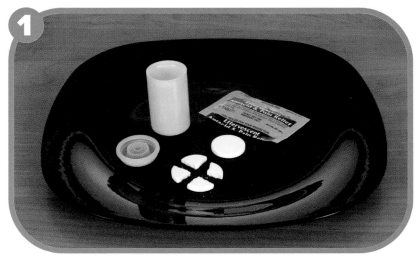

⚠️
SAFETY NOTE
**Have an adult help you
with this experiment!**

MATERIALS

**Alka-Seltzer
Tablets**

**Film
Canister
With a
Snap-On
Lid**

**Construction
Paper**

Duct Tape

Water

**Watch or
Timer**

Notebook

**Safety
Glasses**

LET'S EXPERIMENT

PART 1:
ALKA-SELTZER POPPER

WEARING your safety glasses, divide an Alka-Seltzer tablet into four equal pieces.

FILL half of the film canister with water.

1

GET ready to time the reaction of Alka-Seltzer and water as soon as you do this next step: Place one of the pieces of Alka-Seltzer tablet into the film canister. Observe what happens and record the time. How long does the chemical reaction last—how long does the liquid keep bubbling? Why do you think the liquid stops bubbling? Jot down your notes, then empty the liquid from the film canister into the trash can.

REPEAT the experiment, but this time, place the lid on the canister right after you drop in the piece of Alka-Seltzer. Remember to have a friend or family member start timing the reaction as soon as you drop the piece of Alka-Seltzer into the water. Stand back!

If you're lucky, the lid will pop off and fly into the air at warp speed.

YOU should have two pieces of tablet left. Repeat the experiment using one of the pieces of Alka-Seltzer, but this time you decide the amount of water to put in the film canister. Do you think that will make any difference?

TAKE the remaining piece of Alka-Seltzer and repeat the experiment, except this time, when you put the lid on, turn the canister upside down and observe. What happens?

PART 2: ALKA-SELTZER LAUNCHER

SEAL the end of the cardboard tube with several pieces of duct tape or use a plastic tube with one end sealed.

DIVIDE an Alka-Seltzer tablet into four equal pieces. Fill half the film canister with water.

NOTE: These next steps have to take place very quickly. Read the next few steps first to make sure you understand what is going to happen.

PLACE one of the pieces of Alka-Seltzer tablet in the film canister and quickly snap the lid on the container.

TURN the film canister upside down and slide it (lid first) into the rocket tube.

POINT the open end of the tube AWAY from yourself and others and wait for the pop. Instead of the lid flying off, the bottom of the film canister shoots out of the tube and flies across the room.

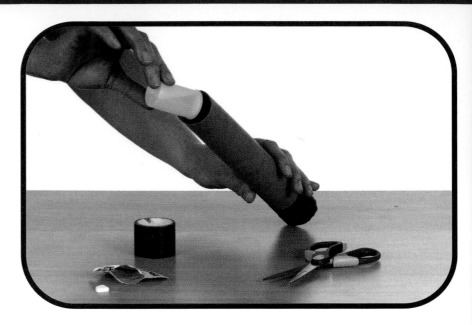

PART 3: ALKA-SELTZER ROCKET

CREATE cardboard fins and a cone and attach them to the cardboard tube as shown to create a rocket.

PREPARE the Alka-Seltzer and water in the film canister as you did in Part 2. Turn it upside down and slide it lid first into the rocket.

PLACE the rocket cone-side up on a flat surface, stand back and wait for the pop. 3...2...1...liftoff!

HOW DOES IT WORK?

The secret is actually hiding in the bubbles you observed. The fizzing you see when you drop an Alka-Seltzer tablet in water is the same sort of fizzing that you see when you mix baking soda and vinegar. Alka-Seltzer contains citric acid and sodium bicarbonate (baking soda). When you drop the tablet in water, the acid and the baking soda react to produce bubbles of carbon dioxide gas.

This gas builds up so much pressure inside the closed film canister that the lid pops off. Since the lid is the path of least resistance for the gas pressure building up inside, it pops off instead of the stronger sides or bottom bursting open.

If you tried the experiment again with water at different temperatures, then you also discovered that temperature plays an important part in the reaction. Warm water speeds up the reaction, while colder water takes longer to build up enough pressure to pop off the lid.

When the buildup of carbon dioxide gas is too great and the lid pops off, Newton's Third Law explains why the film canister flies across the room: For every action, there is an equal and opposite reaction. The lid goes one way and the film canister shoots out of the tube in the opposite direction.

TAKE IT FURTHER

CONSIDER BUILDING rockets out of styrofoam or empty plastic pill bottles. Try decorating your rocket using an array of light materials. With each trial, measure how far the film canister rocket flies across the room. After every launch, write down the amount of water you used in the film canister, the size of the piece of Alka-Seltzer (this should not change) and the distance the film canister traveled. What amount of water mixed with a quarter piece of Alka-Seltzer tablet produces the best rocket fuel? How does the water temperature affect the speed of the reaction? Does warmer or colder water change the distance that the film canister travels? Do you think certain decorations slow down your rocket as it flies through the air?

DID YOU KNOW?

FIRST INTRODUCED IN 1931, ALKA-SELTZER TABLETS CONTAIN THREE INGREDIENTS: ANHYDROUS CITRIC ACID, SODIUM BICARBONATE (BAKING SODA) AND ASPIRIN, OR ACETYLSALICYLIC ACID (ASA). ASIDE FROM HELPING TO EASE AN ASSORTMENT OF MINOR ACHES AND PAINS, IT CAN ALSO BE USED TO CLEAN BASIC THINGS AROUND THE HOUSE LIKE COFFEE MAKERS AND TOILET BOWLS.

WINDBAG WONDERS

LET'S EXPERIMENT

CUT off a section of the bag that is roughly 4 to 5 feet long.

NOTE: A longer section of bag (6 to 8 long) is recommended for any adults who are joining in the fun.

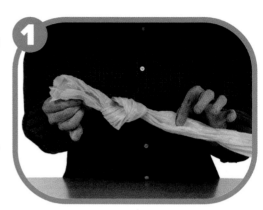

1

2

TIE a knot in one end of the bag. Invite a friend to blow up the bag, keeping track of the number of breaths it takes. Then, squeeze all of the air out of the bag. Explain to your friend that you can blow up the bag in one breath. Chances are, they won't believe you, but that's all part of the surprise!

CAN YOU BLOW UP A HUGE BAG IN ONE BREATH?

MATERIALS

Diaper Genie bag

Scissors

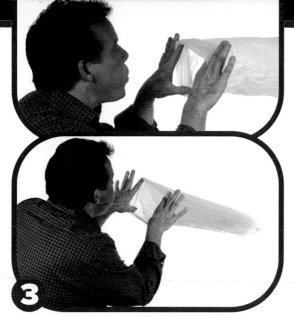

3

HOW DOES IT WORK?

The long bag quickly inflates because air from the atmosphere is drawn into the bag along with the stream of air from your lungs.

In 1738, Daniel Bernoulli concluded that a fast-moving stream of air is surrounded by an area of low atmospheric pressure. In fact, the faster the stream of air moves, the more the air pressure drops around the moving air. When you blow into the bag, higher-pressure air in the atmosphere forces its way into the area of low pressure created by the stream of air moving into the bag from your lungs. In other words, air in the atmosphere is drawn into the long bag at the same time that you are blowing into it.

HAVE your friend assist you by holding onto the closed end of the bag. Hold the open end of the bag approximately 10 inches away from your mouth. Make the opening as wide as you can with the index fingers and thumbs of both hands. Using only one breath, blow a long, steady stream of air into the bag (just as if you were blowing out candles on a birthday cake). You MUST keep your mouth off of the bag (about 10 inches away from the opening) and keep the opening of the bag as large as possible.

IF you do it correctly, you'll see the bag rapidly inflate. The trick is to quickly seal the bag with your hand so that none of the air escapes. Tie a slipknot at the end of the bag or let the air out and try again.

TAKE IT FURTHER

IF YOU really want to challenge your Windbag assembling abilities, check out the jumbo-sized version of this experiment on pg. 100 to put your skills to the test.

DID YOU KNOW?

STEVE SPANGLER PUT BERNOULLI'S PRINCIPLE TO THE TEST AT THE FIRST ANNUAL 9NEWS WEATHER AND SCIENCE DAY AT COORS FIELD IN DENVER, COLORADO, ON MAY 7, 2009. WITH 5,401 PARTICIPANTS BLOWING UP WINDBAGS AT THE EVENT, STEVE SPANGLER AND HIS TEAM WERE AWARDED THE GUINNESS WORLD RECORD FOR THE LARGEST PHYSICS LESSON.

FLOATING AND SINKING ORANGES

WHAT MAKES AN ORANGE SINK OR FLOAT?

MATERIALS

2 Tall Glasses

Water

Oranges (Clementines Work Well)

LET'S EXPERIMENT

1 **FILL** the glasses three-quarters full with water.

FIND two oranges that are just about the same size. As you look closely at the fruit, ask yourself, "Will the oranges float or sink in the water?"

2

3 **DROP** one orange into each glass of water. Observe. As you can see, most oranges will float in water.

4

WOULD the results be any different if you peeled the oranges? Peel the skin off of one of the floating oranges and drop the peeled orange back into the glass of water. Observe.

WAIT...the peeled orange sinks, but the unpeeled orange floats. Removing the peel lessens the weight of the orange, so in theory it should float. Why does peeling the orange make it sink, though?

5

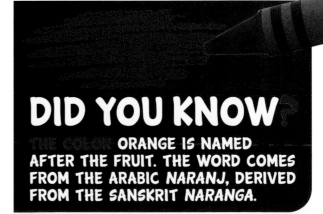

IF you have other types of oranges, repeat the experiment to see if you can find a pattern to help you explain your discovery.

HOW DOES IT WORK?

This experiment is all about **density**—a measure of the mass per unit volume of a substance. Water has a density of 1 gram per milliliter (g/mL). Objects like an unpeeled orange will float in water if their density is less than 1 g/mL. Objects will sink in water if their density is greater than 1 g/mL.

If you weigh the orange on a scale, the orange with a peel is heavier than an orange without a peel. The reason why the orange with the peel (the heavier one) floats is because the peel is porous and filled with tiny air pockets which help increase the **buoyancy** of the orange. This increase in buoyancy helps the orange become less dense than the water, so the orange will float. Think of the pockets of air in the orange peel like tiny flotation devices for the orange. Removing the peel from the orange makes it lighter, but you are also removing those tiny air pocket flotation devices—the orange without the peel is more dense than water and it sinks.

DID YOU KNOW?

THE COLOR **ORANGE IS NAMED AFTER THE FRUIT. THE WORD COMES FROM THE ARABIC** NARANJ, **DERIVED FROM THE SANSKRIT** NARANGA.

FLYING TOILET PAPER

⚠️ **SAFETY NOTE**

Have an adult help you with this experiment!

MATERIALS

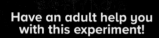

Sheet of Paper

Toilet Paper (The Thinner, the Better)

Leaf Blower

Duct Tape

Paint Roller

Wooden Dowel or Piece of PVC Pipe About 12 Inches (30 cm) Long (Optional)

LET'S EXPERIMENT

HOLD the short edge of a sheet of paper near your lips. Allow the paper to hang down as you blow over the top surface of the paper. Why does the paper rise up? Try blowing air underneath the paper and observe. The paper lifts up just as it did when you blew over the top. How does that work?

1

UNWIND two or three squares from the toilet paper roll and let them hang freely.

HOLD the roll to your chin and blow over the top of the paper just as you did with the sheet of paper. Once again, the paper rises.

GRAB the leaf blower and plug it in. Place the toilet paper on the paint roller and unroll a few squares. Make sure to allow the unrolled tissue to hang loosely off the roll.

2

IF your paint roller has an extender, attach it to the handle of the roller and use the duct tape to secure the extender to the underside of the leaf blower. The paint roller should be horizontal to the mouth of the blower. If your roller doesn't have an extender, attach a wooden dowel to it with duct tape, then secure the dowel to the underside of the blower.

HOLD your leaf blower as if you're about the use it. Make sure the paint roller is horizontal to the ground with the toilet paper unrolling away from you. Turn on the leaf blower. If you've attached the paint roller correctly, the air stream should pass over the top of the surface of the roll.

THE hanging tissue immediately rises and the roll begins to unroll quickly—the entire roll of tissue will unspool and become airborne in a matter of seconds. After doing this experiment, either 1) roll the toilet paper back up, or 2) place the big pile of toilet paper in a garbage bag and keep it in the bathroom to use as needed. Just don't throw it away!

HOW DOES IT WORK?

This experiment is an example of Bernoulli's Principle. Daniel Bernoulli, an 18th century Swiss mathematician, discovered that the faster air flows over the surface of something, the less the air pushes on that surface, resulting in lower pressure.

Blowing under the sheet sufficiently increases the air pressure, causing the paper to lift. Blowing over the top of the sheet lowers the air pressure, allowing the ambient pressure under the sheet to lift it.

The same explanation holds true for the flying toilet paper. Fast-moving air molecules from the leaf blower rushing over the top of the toilet paper exerts less pressure than the air molecules under the toilet paper. At that velocity, the pressure on the upper side of the tissue is reduced dramatically. The relatively greater air pressure beneath the toilet paper supplies the upward force, or lift, that enables the roll to quickly unroll. All of that fast-moving air from the leaf blower propels the toilet paper forward, causing it to unroll rapidly once it takes flight.

DID YOU KNOW?

THE AIR FROM AN ELECTRIC HANDHELD LEAF BLOWER CAN TRAVEL AT SPEEDS EXCEEDING 190 MILES PER HOUR.

TEA BAG ROCKET

MATERIALS

Tea Bag (Bigelow Tea Bags Work Well)

Dinner Plate

Scissors

Matches

Pliers

Handheld Vacuum Cleaner

LET'S EXPERIMENT

1 **OPEN** the tea bag wrapper and remove the tea bag. Use pliers or really strong fingernails to remove the metal staple at the top of the tea bag. Completely unfold the tea bag.

2 **CUT** off both ends of the tea bag and discard the tea.

3 **THE** empty tea bag is actually in the shape of a flattened cylinder. Poke your fingers into the center of the tea bag to reshape it into a cylinder that can stand vertically on one end.

PLACE the tea bag tube on a dinner plate.

HAVE an adult light the top of the tea bag with a match, then stand back and watch the flame burn down. When the tea bag tube has burned down to the very bottom, the ashes will lift off into the air.

4

5

BE careful not to touch the ash until you are certain the fire is completely out. Have a handheld vacuum cleaner handy to suck up the ashes before they ever hit the ground.

HOW DOES IT WORK?

As the tea bag burns, the flame heats the molecules of air inside the tea bag cylinder, which begin to rise since hot air is less dense than cold air. The tea bag continues to burn until nothing is left but a delicate ash frame. Since the ash is so lightweight, the force of the rising hot air is strong enough to lift the ash into the air.

The surrounding cooler air also helps to give the ash lift by a process called convection. As the hot air starts to rise, the cooler surrounding air rushes in to fill the void. This sets up a movement of air called a convection current, which is caused by the expansion of a solid, liquid or gas as its temperature rises.

DID YOU KNOW?

CONVECTION CURRENTS OCCUR IN THE ATMOSPHERE ABOVE WARM LAND MASSES OR SEAS, GIVING RISE TO SEA BREEZES AND LAND BREEZES. IN THE HOT, SOLID ROCK OF THE EARTH'S MANTLE, THESE CURRENTS HELP DRIVE THE MOVEMENT OF THE RIGID PLATES MAKING UP THE EARTH'S SURFACE.

THE TRUST PENDULUM

MATERIALS

Tennis Ball

Duct Tape

Long Piece of String

LET'S EXPERIMENT

MAKE a pendulum by taping a tennis ball to a long piece of string that's attached to the ceiling. When you pull the ball back, there should be enough room for it to swing out and come back to you without hitting anything. Scout a location in your home or garage where you can safely hang the tennis ball pendulum. Ideally, you'll want your subject's back against a wall so that the they won't be tempted to move out of the way of the tennis ball that's flying towards their head.

POSITION a friend or family member against the wall and pull the tennis ball back to their nose. Make sure the ball is touching their nose.

THE key is for them to stay perfectly still. Tell them to be brave. DO NOT give the ball an extra push when you release it or you just might be surprised. 3...2...1... Release the ball!

You'd think the ball would swing back and hit them in the nose, but it doesn't!

ASK yourself: "Why does the ball stop short of making contact with their face?" Then read on.

HOW DOES IT WORK?

According to the **Law of Conservation of Energy**, energy may change from one form to another, but any object or system can never have more energy than what is added to it. When you lift the tennis ball up to your friend's nose, you supply the tennis ball with **potential energy** (stored energy) due to gravity. How high you lift the ball represents the total amount of energy added to the ball. As the ball is released, gravity accelerates the ball downward toward the ground, decreasing the amount of potential energy and increasing the amount of **kinetic energy** (energy of motion) as the ball gains speed.

As the ball reaches the bottom of its arc, all of its potential energy is changed into kinetic energy. As it begins to climb on the upswing, the opposite occurs: The ball slows down, decreasing the amount of kinetic energy as it changes back into potential energy. At the top of the arc, the ball stops momentarily, with all of the energy changed back into potential energy, before the process repeats itself in the opposite direction. In a perfect system, the ball would reach the original starting height, hitting your subject in the face. However, in each successive swing, friction causes the ball to lose a small amount of its kinetic energy. The lower height in each swing represents the amount of energy lost due to friction in the string and the pendulum having to push through the air as it moves back and forth. Over time, the ball moves less and less until it returns to the bottom of the arc, where the pendulum has lost all of its potential energy.

TAKE IT FURTHER

PUT YOUR knowledge of physics to the test by experimenting with your own potential and kinetic energy. If you have a tire swing or simply a knotted rope hanging from a tree in your backyard, see how far you can safely swing on the rope without falling or losing your grip. This is especially fun if you have a pool or live near a lake! Try it with a friend and see just how far you go.

DID YOU KNOW?

ACCORDING TO **THE INTERNATIONAL TENNIS FEDERATION, A TENNIS BALL SHOULD WEIGH BETWEEN 1.975 AND 2.095 OUNCES. MODERN DAY TENNIS BALLS ARE HOLLOW AND MADE FROM FELT-COVERED RUBBER, BUT IN THE 1870S, THEY WERE MADE ENTIRELY OF RUBBER.**

WATER BOTTLE EGG SEPARATOR

⚠️ **SAFETY NOTE**

Make sure to wash your hands after handling raw eggs. If you plan to eat your colorful creation, make sure to wash the plastic water bottle before using.

MATERIALS

Raw Eggs

Empty Plastic Water Bottle

Plate or Bowl

Food Coloring

LET'S EXPERIMENT

1 **CRACK** an egg onto a plate or into a bowl, being careful not to accidentally break the yolk. The challenge is to separate the yolk (the yellow part) from the egg white (the clear, gooey stuff) without breaking the yolk.

HOLD the empty plastic water bottle upside down over the egg yolk. Gently squeeze the sides of the bottle slightly to force out some of the air that's in the bottle. Don't squeeze too much—a little squeeze works great.

2

3 **TOUCH** the mouth of the bottle to the yellow egg yolk and slowly release your hold on the bottle. Observe. The egg yolk gets pushed up into the bottle.

ONCE the egg yolk is in the bottle, tip the bottle sideways and pull it away from the egg whites that remain on the plate or bowl. If you want to put the egg yolk someplace for safekeeping, turn the bottle upside down over another plate or bowl. The yolk will slide down into the neck of the bottle. Gently squeeze the bottle and the yolk will pop out!

HOW DOES IT WORK?

The scientific secret to this kitchen hack is nothing but air pressure. This empty-looking bottle is actually filled with air. Squeezing the sides of the bottle forces out some of the air, and when the mouth of the bottle touches the egg yolk, it forms a seal that keeps the outside air from rushing back into the bottle. When you release, the air pressure on the outside of the bottle is greater than the air pressure inside the bottle. The higher pressure outside the bottle actually pushes the egg yolk up into the bottle because of the airtight seal that is formed between the yolk and the bottle.

If you've ever squeezed an empty water bottle and placed your tongue over the top, the bottle will stick to your tongue when you release the squeeze. The "sucking" force that you feel is actually the air pressure outside the bottle trying to push your tongue into the bottle.

TAKE IT FURTHER

CRACK SEVERAL eggs into a bowl and use the water bottle trick to separate the yolks from the egg whites without breaking the yolks. Add a few drops of food coloring (or more, for a brighter color) to the egg whites and beat them with a fork. Melt some butter in a frying pan and pour the colorful egg whites into the pan. Carefully pour the egg yolks into the middle of the pan and fry up the eggs. Your guests will wonder how you colored the egg whites without breaking the yolks.

DID YOU KNOW?

ABOUT 57 PERCENT OF AN EGG'S PROTEIN IS CONTAINED IN AN EGG WHITE.

UNBELIEVABLE FLOATIES

⚠️
SAFETY NOTE

Have an adult help you with this experiment! Never point a stream of air at a person or an animal.

MATERIALS

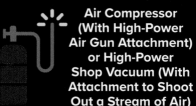

Air Compressor (With High-Power Air Gun Attachment) or High-Power Shop Vacuum (With Attachment to Shoot Out a Stream of Air)

Carrot   **Screwdriver**

OTHER OBJECTS TO USE

- **Raw hot dog, small cucumber, apple, orange or other fruits and vegetables with a curved top**
- **Plastic baseball bat, soup ladle, plastic soda bottle, plastic gallon milk jug, plastic bowl**
- **Plastic ball, golf ball, baseball, softball, racquetball, beach ball, Wiffle ball**

LET'S EXPERIMENT

NOTE: In all of our testing, an air compressor with a high-power air blower nozzle works best for this experiment. However, it's possible to use a shop vacuum cleaner by reattaching the hose to the place where the air comes out and using a nozzle that funnels the air into a smaller stream. Either way, you'll want to create a steady stream of air.

1

FIRE up the air compressor and attach the high-power air gun nozzle. You might need to wait for the air compressor to build up pressure. If you're using a shop vacuum cleaner, attach the nozzle to make a powerful stream of air.

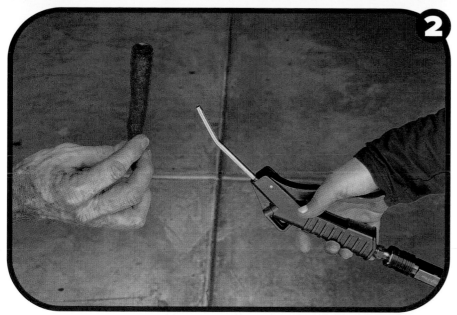

2

FIND a medium-sized carrot. Carrots work well because you can reshape the carrot top by scraping it on the cement if you're outside or by carefully carving it with a knife.

POSITION the nozzle so that the stream of air is at an angle (not pointed straight up). You're going to shoot the stream of high-powered air from the side instead of straight up from under the object.

PLACE the carrot in the stream of air and test to see if it will float when you let go. If not, change the angle of the stream, or position the carrot closer to the air, or maybe you need a little more or less air—there are lots of variables and you'll need to keep trying... but we know you can make the carrot float.

3

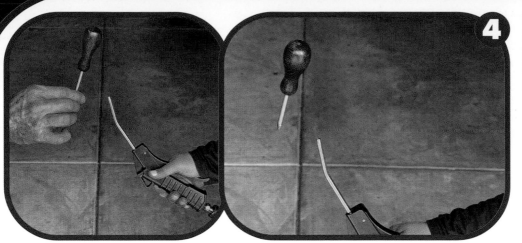

NEXT, try floating a screwdriver. Position it so that the curved handle is at the top. Observe. It also floats!

TRY some of the other objects from the list (in these images, we're using a shop vacuum). You've probably noticed by now that all of the objects from the list have a rounded top. That's very important because the fast-moving stream of air must be able to flow over the top of the object. Try a ball like a beach ball, baseball or softball. Hold the nozzle so the stream of air is pointing straight up.

HOW DOES IT WORK?

Depending on the object you're trying to float and where the stream of air is positioned, there are two scientific principles to explore.

The Coandă effect, named for Romanian inventor Henri Coandă, is the tendency of a stream of air (he used the word fluid) to stay attached to a convex surface rather than follow a straight line in its original direction.

It's easy to see how the Coandă effect works by attaching a piece of string to the end of the air nozzle. The string follows the path of the fast-moving air molecules as they hug the curved (convex) surface of the object. You can see how cutting off the rounded top of the carrot completely changes the way the air molecules flow. So, when air flows over the curved top, the air pressure is reduced above the object and it's the stationary air pressure underneath them that holds the objects up.

Round floating objects (e.g., a beach ball, softball, etc.), on the other hand, illustrate Bernoulli's Principle. Daniel Bernoulli,

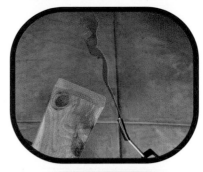

an 18th-century Swiss mathematician, discovered something quite unusual about moving air. He found that the faster air flows over the surface of something, the less the air pushes on that surface (and so the lower its pressure). The stream of air shoots up from below the ball, flows around the outside of the ball and, if you position the ball carefully, flows evenly around each side. Gravity pulls the ball downward while the pressure below the ball from the moving air forces it upward. This means that all the forces acting on the ball are balanced and the ball hovers in midair.

WINDBAG WONDERS (THE JUMBO-SIZED VERSION)

LET'S EXPERIMENT

GRAB your friends and family and announce they have five minutes to work together to build the largest freestanding Wind Tube structure they possibly can. The structure must be held up only by the Windbags themselves—no one can hold up the structure.

TAKE THE EXPERIMENT FROM PG. 80 TO THE NEXT LEVEL!

MATERIALS

**Windbags
(See Pg. 80 for
Instructions)**

Rubber Bands

1

LOOP two rubber bands together to form a figure eight.

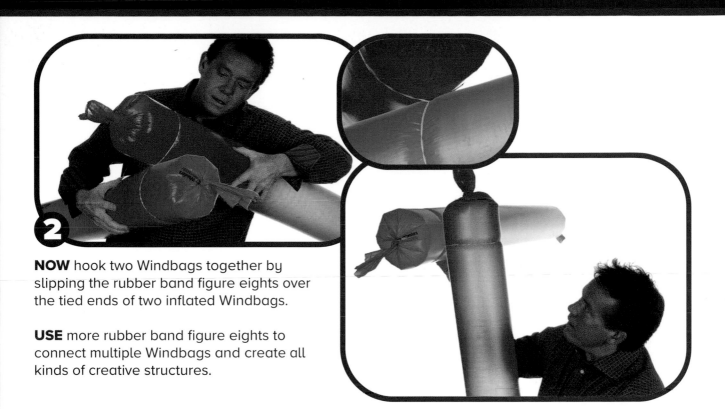

2

NOW hook two Windbags together by slipping the rubber band figure eights over the tied ends of two inflated Windbags.

USE more rubber band figure eights to connect multiple Windbags and create all kinds of creative structures.

IT'S a great team-building activity for kids and adults alike.

3

HOW DOES IT WORK?

For more info on why this activity works, turn to pg. 81!

DID YOU KNOW?

AMONG OTHER

THINGS, BERNOULLI'S PRINCIPLE EXPLAINS HOW AIRPLANES CAN FLY, HOW ROOFS CAN BLOW AWAY IN HEAVY WINDS AND HOW A BALL THROWN WITH A SPIN WILL MOVE IN A CURVE.

MIND-BLOWING TRICKS

Your audience will chalk it up to magic, but you know the truth.

BED OF NAILS

IT PAYS TO SMILE

STRAW THROUGH POTATO

DRY ICE CRYSTAL BALL BUBBLE

⚠️

SAFETY NOTE

This experiment must be done with an adult. Dry ice will burn bare skin. Only handle with heavy gloves.

MATERIALS

Safety Glasses

Large Bowl With a Smooth Rim (Smaller Than 12 Inches in Diameter)

Liquid Dish Soap (Dawn Works Well)

Piece of Cloth (18 Inches Long)

Plastic Cup

Dry Ice

Heavy Leather Gloves

LET'S EXPERIMENT

MIX 2 tablespoons (30 mL) of liquid dish soap with 1 tablespoon (15 mL) of water in a plastic cup.

CUT a strip of cloth about 1 inch (2.5 cm) wide and 18 inches (46 cm) long. Soak the cloth in the soapy solution, making sure it is completely submerged.

FILL the bowl halfway with warm water, then put your gloves on.

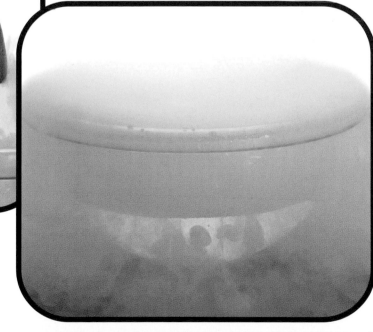

WITH your gloved hands, gently place two or three pieces of dry ice into the water so that a good amount of fog is produced. Once you've added the dry ice, you can remove your gloves.

5

REMOVE the strip of cloth from the soap solution and run your fingers down the cloth to remove the excess soap.

6

WITH one end of the cloth in each hand, stretch the cloth, then slowly pull it across the rim of the bowl.

7

THE GOAL is to create a soap film that stretches across the entire bowl. (It helps to dip your fingers in some water and wet the rim of the bowl before you start.) This can take a little practice until you master the technique. If all else fails, try cutting a new strip of cloth from a different type of fabric (an old T-shirt works well) or change the soap solution by adding more water.

Once you've got the soap film in place, observe. A massive bubble forms! Take a moment to marvel at your creation. If you poke it, the bubble will pop!

HOW DOES IT WORK?

When you drop a piece of dry ice in a bowl of water, the gas that you see is a combination of carbon dioxide (CO_2) and water vapor, meaning it's actually a cloud of tiny water droplets. The thin layer of soap film stretched across the rim of the bowl traps the expanding cloud to create a giant bubble. When the water gets colder than 50 degrees F, the dry ice stops making fog but continues to sublimate and bubble. Just replace the cold water with warm water and you're back in business.

DID YOU KNOW?

DRY ICE WAS FIRST OBSERVED IN 1835 BY FRENCH INVENTOR ADRIEN-JEAN-PIERRE THILORIER AFTER HE OPENED A CONTAINER OF LIQUID CARBON DIOXIDE. IT IS EXTREMELY COLD (-109.3 DEGREES F) AND CAN LEAD TO FROSTBITE WHEN HANDLED IMPROPERLY. THAT'S WHY YOU NEED GLOVES!

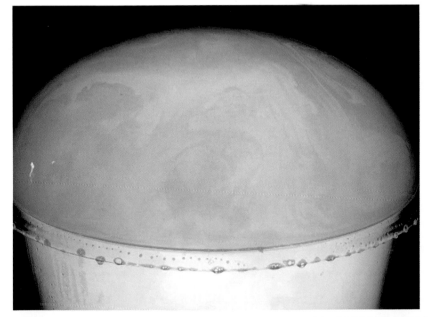

TAKE IT FURTHER

IF YOU accidentally get soap in the bowl of water, many fog-filled bubbles will start to emerge from the bowl. This produces a great effect. Place a waterproof flashlight in the bowl along with the dry ice so that the light shines up through the fog. Draw the cloth across the rim to create the soap film lid and, if you are inside, turn off the lights. The crystal bubbles will emit an eerie glow and you'll be able to see the fog churning inside the transparent bubble walls. When the giant bubble bursts, the cloud falls to the floor, creating an outburst of oohs and ahhs from anyone watching!

FLOATING WATER

IS IT POSSIBLE TO TURN A GLASS FILLED WITH WATER UPSIDE DOWN WITHOUT SPILLING?

MATERIALS

Plastic Cup or Drinking Glass

Index Card or Old Playing Card

Large Bowl or Sink

LET'S EXPERIMENT

NOTE: Make sure the index card or playing card is large enough to completely cover the mouth of the glass.

1 FILL the glass or plastic cup to the top with water.

2 COVER the cup with the card, making sure the card completely covers the mouth of the container.

3 READ this next part before you do it: Keep your hand on the card and turn the cup upside down. Hold the cup over a bowl or sink just in case you spill.

Slowly take your hand away and the card will stay in place... and so should the water.

WHEN you're done, put your hand back on the card and return the cup to its upright position.

You can repeat this experiment, as long as the card doesn't become completely soaked and begin to fall apart.

HOW DOES IT WORK?

Air molecules in the atmosphere exert pressure on everything. At sea level, for example, air molecules in the atmosphere exert almost 15 pounds of pressure per square inch of surface area.

When you first turn the cup upside down, the pressure of the air inside the cup and the air pressure outside the cup are equal. If you look closely, however, you'll notice some water leaks out between the card and the cup because the force of **gravity** naturally pulls down on the water. This causes the volume of air (the space above the water inside the cup) to increase slightly. Even though the amount of air above the water stays the same, the volume occupied by the air is now greater and the air pressure inside the cup decreases. The pressure of the air outside the cup is now greater than the pressure inside the cup and the card stays in place. This is because the water creates an airtight seal between the rim of the cup and the card.

When the seal is broken, air enters the cup and equalizes the pressure, and gravity pushes the water out. Poking a thumbtack-sized hole in the cup allows air to seep into the cup from the outside. The pressure of the air molecules inside and outside the cup stays the same, gravity takes over, the card falls and the water spills.

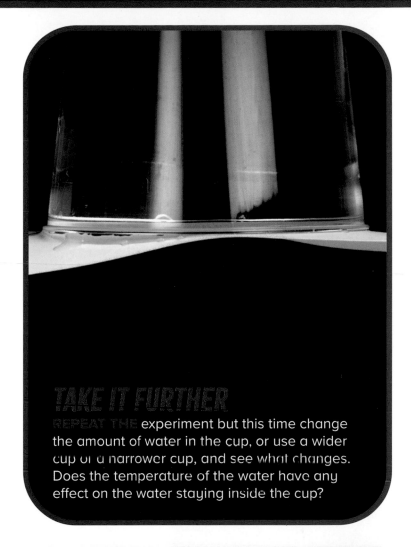

TAKE IT FURTHER

REPEAT THE experiment but this time change the amount of water in the cup, or use a wider cup or a narrower cup, and see what changes. Does the temperature of the water have any effect on the water staying inside the cup?

DID YOU KNOW?

IF YOU'VE **CLIMBED A MOUNTAIN, YOU KNOW BREATHING IS MORE DIFFICULT AT HIGHER ALTITUDES. AIR PRESSURE IS LOW AT HIGH ALTITUDES—WHEN IT'S HIGH, LIKE AT SEA LEVEL, THE PRESSURE KEEPS OXYGEN MOLECULES PACKED TOGETHER, AND IT'S EASIER FOR US TO CATCH OUR BREATH. BUT AT HIGH ALTITUDES, OXYGEN MOLECULES SPREAD OUT, AND IT TAKES MORE WORK TO GET THE OXYGEN WE NEED.**

STRAW THROUGH POTATO

MATERIALS

2 or More Stiff Straws

Large Raw Potato

LET'S EXPERIMENT

GATHER a group of your friends and family and announce you're going to stab a potato with a straw—without breaking the straw. As you hold the potato with your non-writing hand, keep your fingers on the front and your thumb on the back and not on the top and bottom. You don't want to stab yourself! Grab the straw with your writing hand and cap the top end with your thumb.

1

HOLD on firmly to the straw and the potato. Read this next step before you do it: With a quick, sharp stab, drive the straw into and part-way out of the narrow end of the spud (not the fatter, middle part).

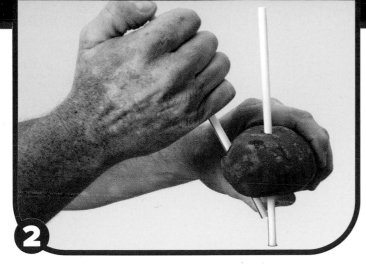
2

YOUR audience will be impressed and will want to try it. Tell them to hold the spud the way you did so they don't stab a finger or thumb with the straw. They may not know the secret, so don't give it away just yet. Let them try to figure it out.

TAKE IT FURTHER

USING YOUR favorite fruits and vegetables, repeat the experiment and check your results.

HOW DOES IT WORK?

The secret isn't the straw itself but what's inside the straw—air. Placing your thumb over the end of the straw traps the air inside. The air molecules compress and give the straw strength, which in turn keeps the sides from bending as you jam the straw through the potato. The trapped, compressed air makes the straw strong enough to cut through the skin, pass through the potato and exit out the other side. Without your thumb covering the hole, the air is simply pushed out of the straw and the straw crumples and breaks as it hits the hard potato surface. Be sure to keep your fingers out of the way. After you stab with the straw, take a look at the end that passed through the potato and see how much you were able to remove.

DID YOU KNOW?
THERE ARE **MORE THAN 200 TYPES OF POTATO AVAILABLE IN THE U.S. ALONE.**

DRIPPING CANDLE SEESAW

CAN TWO LIT CANDLES MAKE A SEESAW MOVE?

⚠️ **SAFETY NOTE**
Have an adult help you with this experiment!

MATERIALS

Pointed Tip Scissors

2 Small Birthday Candles

3 Small Paper Clips

Ruler

Small Plastic Container

Thumbtack

2 Straws

Matches

Newspaper (Just In Case)

LET'S EXPERIMENT

1

USING the pointed end of the scissors, poke a hole into the center of the bottom of the small plastic cup. The hole should be just big enough to allow the end of one of the straws to slide through. Insert the straw. Turn the cup upside down and place it so that the mouth of the cup is flat against the table.

USING the ruler, find the middle of the remaining straw. Then use the thumbtack to poke a hole all the way through the straw and out the other side. Try to keep the thumbtack level as you pierce the straw.

TAKE one of the paper clips and straighten out the smaller loop so that it is almost straight (see the photos on the right). Take the end of the straightened side and bend it upward. The shape you end up with should look like an L connected to a J.

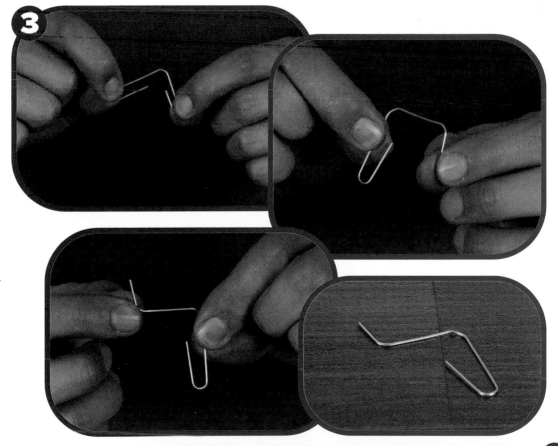

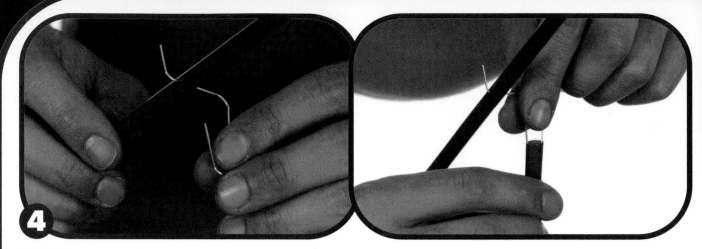

4

SLIDE the L end of the bent paper clip through the straw where you punched the holes. Slide the paper clip so that the straw is at the bottom of the L, then take the J side of the bent paper clip and insert it into the top of the straw opposite the cup. Your apparatus should look like a seesaw now.

INSERT the flat non-wick end of each candle into the two ends of the seesaw straw. To hold each candle in place, slide a paper clip across the face of the straw, enclosing both it and the candle.

5

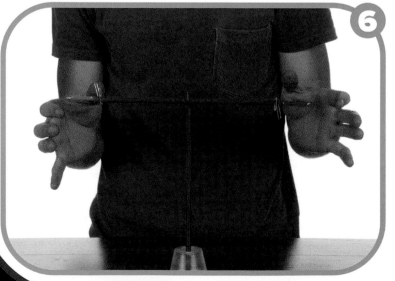

6 **BALANCE** the seesaw by sliding the two candles in or out of the straw. Rest the entire setup on a piece of newspaper to catch the wax drippings.

ASK your friends or family, "What will happen when I light one of the candles?" Give every person a chance to share his or her predictions, then light one of the candles and observe.

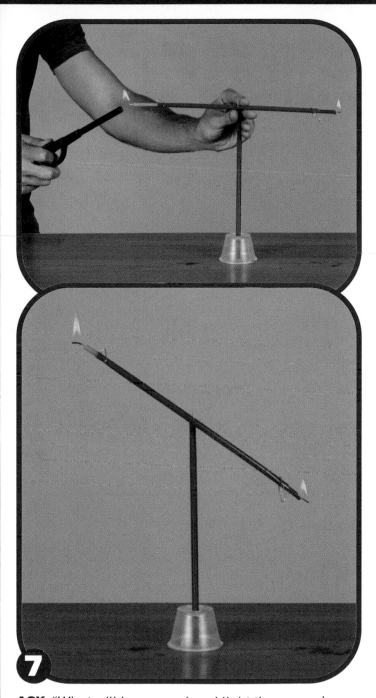

7

HOW DOES IT WORK?

The rotational action of the Candle Seesaw comes from the changing mass of the candles—potential energy that gets turned into rotational kinetic energy.

When the candles begin to drip wax, they lose potential energy. If both candles dripped wax at exactly the same rate, there would be no movement, but this happens only when both candles are lit at exactly the same time. As the heavier candle in the seesaw moves downward, the angled flame causes the candle wax to melt faster and drip more. When the dripping candle loses enough mass, it also loses potential energy and moves upward (just like a seesaw). The candle on the other end moves downward, the angled flame melts the wax, which drops onto the paper, and the seesaw is set back into motion. The careful observer is quick to point out that the height of the swing (otherwise known as the **amplitude**) increases with each cycle. Eventually, the kinetic energy (or the energy of motion) is great enough to produce a full rotation.

ASK, "What will happen when I light the second candle?" Light it and observe. After about 15 seconds, the candles will start to move up and down in a seesaw-like motion. As time goes on, the swing of the straw gets greater and greater until eventually you get a full rotation.

GENIE IN THE BOTTLE

MATERIALS

2 Opaque Glass Soda Bottles

NOTE
Use opaque bottles when performing this trick so no one guesses the secret! We used clear bottles to show you how this works.

2 Pieces of Rope

Small Ball (Must Fit Inside the Mouth of the Bottle) or Balled-Up Aluminum Foil

LET'S EXPERIMENT

1

GATHER your friends and family to perform this trick, but before you do, secretly place the small ball in your bottle. (The bottle that you give to a friend to use will not have a ball.)

START the magic trick by telling everyone the incredible story that there's a genie in the bottle and explain how you can use a rope to wake up the genie. Hand the bottle without the ball to your friend along with a piece of rope. This leaves the other bottle and rope for you to use.

PLACE the rope into your bottle. Have your friend do the same.

WHILE holding the rope in place, turn the bottle upside down. As you do this, the ball will secretly fall into the neck of the bottle.

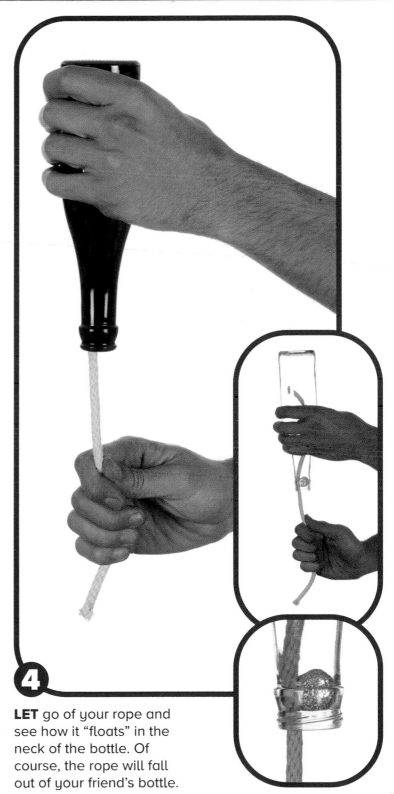

LET go of your rope and see how it "floats" in the neck of the bottle. Of course, the rope will fall out of your friend's bottle.

5

HOLD onto the end of the rope while turning the bottle right side up and let go of the bottle. To everyone's amazement, the bottle is magically hooked onto the rope. Hey...it's the genie holding onto the rope, right?

WHEN you want the "genie" to let go, push the rope back into the bottle to release the ball. This will allow you to pull the rope out of the bottle.

6

HOW DOES IT WORK?

Aside from using misdirection to keep the audience from seeing the ball in your bottle, the force that makes this trick possible is called friction. Friction is the force or resistance that fights against the movement of one object or surface against another object or surface. When the rubber ball gets lodged between the rope and the bottle, it forms a wedge that keeps the rope from falling out and even lets you dangle the bottle from the rope. When you push the rope downward slightly, the resistance is removed, the ball drops into the bottle, and the rope can be easily removed from the bottle.

TAKE IT FURTHER

YOU CAN secretly "steal" the ball out of your bottle by placing your hand on the top of the bottle and turning it upside down (while pretending to inspect the bottom of the bottle). This will allow the ball to secretly fall into your hand. Now you can offer to trade bottles and ropes with your friend. When they're not looking, sneak the ball into your bottle and do the trick again!

DID YOU KNOW?

ACCORDING TO **RESEARCH, IT WOULD TAKE 4,000 YEARS FOR A GLASS BOTTLE TO DECOMPOSE. GLASS-MAKING DATES BACK TO AROUND 3500 B.C. IN EGYPT AND EASTERN MESOPOTAMIA.**

CORK IN A WINE BOTTLE PUZZLE

HOW DO YOU GET THE CORK OUT OF THE BOTTLE WITHOUT RUINING THE CORK, THE BOTTLE OR BOTH?

MATERIALS

Empty Wine Bottle

Cork

Rubber Mallet

Small Stick

Handkerchief or Cloth Napkin

LET'S EXPERIMENT

PUT the cork in the wine bottle: Push it into the top of the bottle, then use a rubber mallet to gently push it as far into the bottle as you can. You could also turn the bottle over and tap the cork lightly on a table until the cork is even with the top of the bottle.

USE a small stick or handle to push the cork all the way into the bottle. Now you have what's called an "Impossible Bottle"—a bottle that contains something that appears to be too large to fit through the neck of the bottle and that won't easily come out. Some Impossible Bottles feature ships, decks of cards, tennis balls, scissors, knotted ropes and many other unusual items inside.

3 **CALL** a friend over and present them with this challenge: "Can you pull the cork out of the bottle without destroying it or the bottle?" Remind them that they can't set the cork on fire or put something down into the bottle that will break the cork into smaller pieces or break the bottle. Let them hold the bottle and ponder the challenge for a while.

ONCE they've given up, push the handkerchief down into the bottle, leaving about half the handkerchief sticking out of the bottle so that you can grab onto it.

4

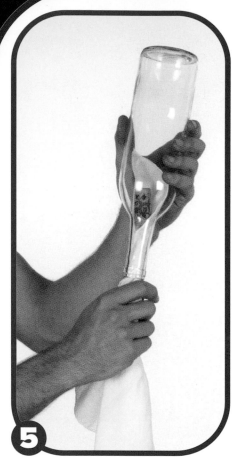

5

TIP the bottle upside down and gently shake it until the cork is lodged between the handkerchief and the inside of the bottle near the neck.

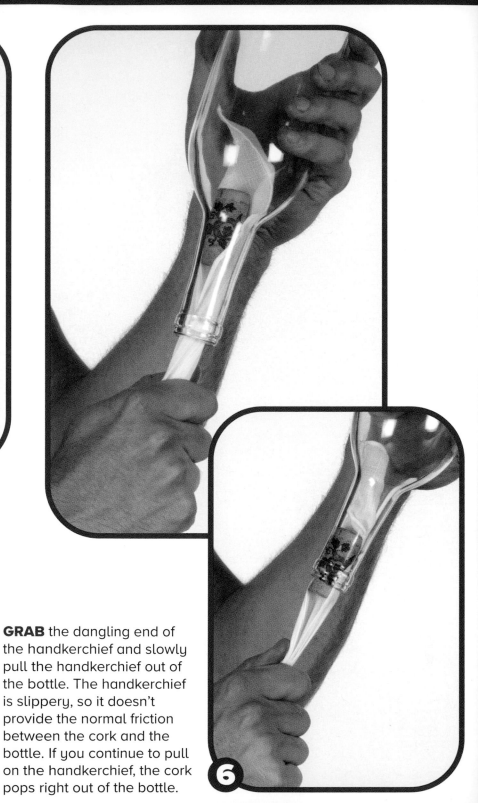

6

GRAB the dangling end of the handkerchief and slowly pull the handkerchief out of the bottle. The handkerchief is slippery, so it doesn't provide the normal friction between the cork and the bottle. If you continue to pull on the handkerchief, the cork pops right out of the bottle.

HOW DOES IT WORK?

The cork comes out of the bottle due to the simple science of friction. Wine manufacturers use corks in bottles because the friction between the cork and the glass forms a nice tight seal. If you remove the friction (by using the handkerchief), you can very easily pull the cork back out of the bottle.

TAKE IT FURTHER

SEE IF you can remove a cork from an empty wine bottle using a produce bag from the grocery store instead of a napkin or handkerchief. What other items could you use to try to get the cork out of the bottle?

DID YOU KNOW?

CORK IS **HARVESTED FROM THE CORK OAK, A TREE THAT, ON AVERAGE, CAN LIVE FOR ABOUT 200 YEARS.**

IT PAYS TO SMILE

LET'S EXPERIMENT

MATERIALS

**Crisp, New
$1 Bill**

NOTE: The secret is in the way you fold the dollar bill.

START with George Washington's portrait facing you. Make a "mountain fold" through the middle of George's left eye. In origami terms, this means to fold the bill away from you.

MAKE a second mountain fold through the middle of his right eye. Make sure that these creases are sharp.

MAKE a "valley fold" between the two previous folds so that the crease is between George's eyes and nose. To make a valley fold, fold the bill toward you. Pull on the ends of the bill slightly so that you can see his entire face, but make sure that the folds are still present.

HOLD the portrait side of the bill in front of you with the face tilted upward. Notice how George smiles at you!

SLOWLY begin to tilt the bill downward, as if George were looking at the floor. Don't take your eyes off George's face—his smile will magically turn into a frown.

HOW DOES IT WORK?

The George Washington face-lift is a great example of an optical illusion. The opposing folds cause the features on the face to bend and contort, depending on how you look at them. Although it's one of the simplest activities in this book, it's one you'll find yourself doing over and over again.

TAKE IT FURTHER

USE DIFFERENT dollar bills ($5, $10, $20, $50, even $100) to see if you can alter the emotions of some other presidents. Is Honest Abe hiding a smile?

DID YOU KNOW?

TWO OF **THE MOST WELL-KNOWN ARTISTS WHOSE WORKS INCORPORATED OPTICAL ILLUSIONS INCLUDE M.C. ESCHER AND SALVADOR DALI.**

DRY-ERASE MARKER MAGIC

MATERIALS

Plates With Smooth Surfaces

Dry-Erase Markers (Different Colors)

Water

LET'S EXPERIMENT

1

GRAB your dry-erase markers and make a drawing on your first plate such as a stick figure, a heart or maybe a word. Does it look like the ink is sticking to the surface of the plate?

LET it dry for a couple of seconds and then use a dry finger to wipe across your drawing. Does your finger wipe off the drawing, or can you still see it?

If the drawing came off, make a new drawing. Otherwise, keep the old one.

2

POUR just enough water onto your plate to cover the drawing. Wait and observe. If nothing happens, shake the plate a little bit. What happens to the ink after a while? Does your drawing begin to float and come to life?

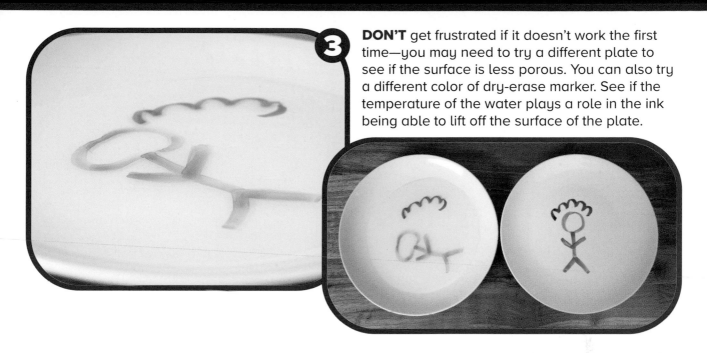

3 **DON'T** get frustrated if it doesn't work the first time—you may need to try a different plate to see if the surface is less porous. You can also try a different color of dry-erase marker. See if the temperature of the water plays a role in the ink being able to lift off the surface of the plate.

HOW DOES IT WORK?

You probably have a whiteboard in your school classroom. To draw on this surface, your teacher uses a dry-erase marker. The writing from these markers can easily be erased from the whiteboard without leaving any marks, but how?

Dry-erase markers contain special ingredients, including a solvent—usually some kind of alcohol—which is used to dissolve the color pigments that determine the marker's color. In addition, a resin is added, which is the key to making the ink erasable. In a dry-erase marker, the resin is an oily silicone polymer, which makes the ink of the marker very slippery and prevents it from sticking to exceptionally smooth, nonporous surfaces such as a whiteboard or glass.

When you draw on such a surface with a dry-erase marker, the solvent that dissolves the ink ingredients evaporates, leaving the color pigment and oily silicone polymer behind. The polymer prevents the color pigment from sticking to the surface.

When you pour a little water on the plate, the water is able to slip underneath the ink. And since the ink is lighter than water, it can float.

TABLECLOTH TRICK

HELP SET THE TABLE, THEN MYSTIFY YOUR FAMILY!

MATERIALS

Smooth or Slick Tablecloth (Without Hems)

Flat Tabletop With Straight Sides

Heavy Dinner Plates, Saucers and Glasses

Don't use your favorite dinnerware for this experiment—it might break!

Look carefully at the bottoms of your cups and plates to make sure that their surfaces are smooth. Plastic cups and plates don't work well because they are so lightweight.

You can also head out to your local fabric store and purchase a 3-foot square piece of fabric (one square yard). You might look for something that has a smooth or slippery surface. Testing various types of cloth is all part of the experimentation process.

LET'S EXPERIMENT

PART of the secret of the trick is learning how to position the tablecloth on the table. The key is to make sure none of the tablecloth

hangs over the edge of the table that's away from you. Keep the excess hanging off the edge of the table that is closest to you.

START with a single dinner plate. Place the dinner plate on top of the tablecloth near the audience-facing edge of the cloth.

THE TRICK is to grab the edge of the tablecloth with both hands and quickly jerk the cloth down and away from the table. The key is the quick, downward motion. Keep saying to yourself, "Pull down, not out." Make sure to pull perpendicular to the table with as little an inclined angle as possible. Also, make sure your palms are facing down.

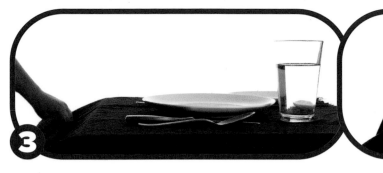

③

RESET the table with the tablecloth, a plate, a bowl, silverware, cups or whatever you've got. Fill your cups with some water and test out your newly acquired tablecloth whipping skills.

NOTE: Practice doesn't necessarily guarantee success. There's always a chance for error, so it might be a good idea to attempt this over a carpeted floor (or outside!).

HOW DOES IT WORK?

The Tablecloth Trick works because of inertia. Sir Issac Newton first described inertia as the tendency of an object at rest to remain at rest or an object in motion to stay in motion until a force acts upon the object. In terms of the Tablecloth Trick, inertia is important because, according to the law, the objects (the stuff on the table) will not move unless an outside force moves them. This is known as Newton's First Law of Motion.

When you pull the cloth, friction acts on the objects in the direction of the pull for a short time. But the force of friction is very small in comparison to the force of inertia for the objects resting on the tablecloth. Filling the glass with water, for example, makes the stunt look more difficult, but the additional weight actually makes it easier! This is because the additional weight of the water (or anything you put on the dinner plate) increases the objects' inertia. The greater the inertia of the objects on the table, the easier it is to quickly pull the tablecloth out from under the dinnerware.

TAKE IT FURTHER

INSTEAD OF testing out different plates, bowls and glasses, try experimenting with different masses on the plates. Make the plate or bowl heavier by adding a piece of fruit or something with some weight. Stack a glass on top of the plates. Is it easier or harder to whip off the tablecloth?

DID YOU KNOW?

ALBERT EINSTEIN **DEVELOPED THE THEORY OF SPECIAL RELATIVITY BASED ON GALILEO'S OBSERVATION THAT IT'S IMPOSSIBLE TO TELL THE DIFFERENCE BETWEEN AN OBJECT IN MOTION AND AN OBJECT AT REST WITHOUT AN OUTSIDE FRAME OF REFERENCE.**

STOP AND GO PENDULUMS

MATERIALS

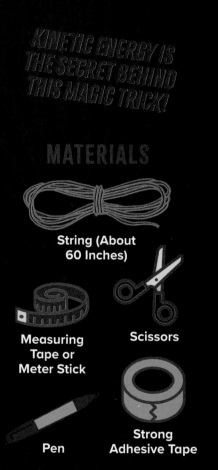

String (About 60 Inches)

Measuring Tape or Meter Stick

Scissors

Pen

Strong Adhesive Tape

Weights to Hang From the String (2 Identical— But Not Too Lightweight— Objects Like Tennis Balls or Plastic Balls)

LET'S EXPERIMENT

NOTE: You will need to find a very sturdy place to hang this pendulum system, like the top of a doorway. It's important to use strong tape, but make sure the tape will not ruin the paint or the wood when you remove it.

①

STUDY the photo of the pendulums hanging from the string to get a better idea of how this works. Cut a piece of string that measures 36 inches (92 cm), then cut two pieces of string that measure 20 inches (51 cm). It's important that these last two pieces of string are exactly the same size.

USE the pen to mark 14 inches (36 cm) from each end of the longer string. This is the point where you will attach the two smaller pieces of string. Make sure the knots are tight to keep the strings from sliding.

ATTACH the weights to the ends of the smaller strings with strong tape. Try to make sure they end up as close to the same length as possible.

HANG this "double pendulum" from a place that is sturdy, like a doorway. You don't want too much slack in the string. Try to keep the ends of the string about 34 inches (86 cm) apart and attach the string so that the ends are level.

MAKE sure both pendulums are at rest. GENTLY pull back the pendulum on the left about 12 inches (30 cm) or so and let go. If you pull back too far and swing the pendulum too hard, it will not work. Observe.

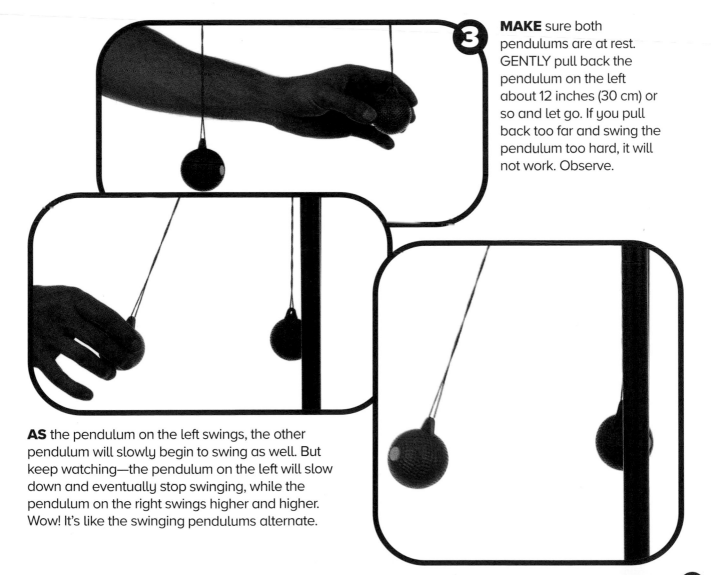

AS the pendulum on the left swings, the other pendulum will slowly begin to swing as well. But keep watching—the pendulum on the left will slow down and eventually stop swinging, while the pendulum on the right swings higher and higher. Wow! It's like the swinging pendulums alternate.

GRADUALLY, the pendulum on the right will slow down and stop swinging while the pendulum on the left will begin to swing. Eventually, both pendulums will lose energy and come to rest.

4

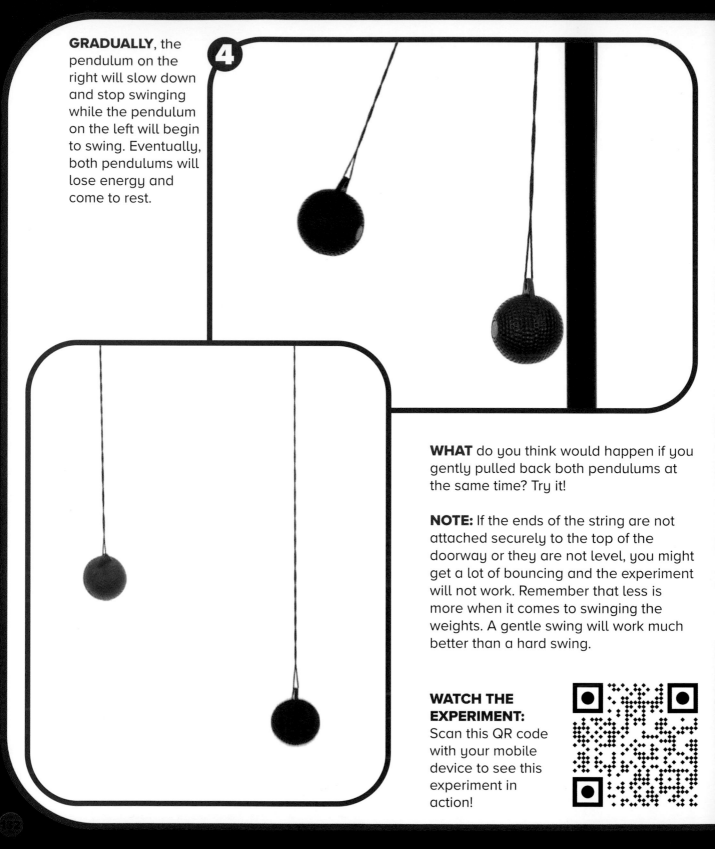

WHAT do you think would happen if you gently pulled back both pendulums at the same time? Try it!

NOTE: If the ends of the string are not attached securely to the top of the doorway or they are not level, you might get a lot of bouncing and the experiment will not work. Remember that less is more when it comes to swinging the weights. A gentle swing will work much better than a hard swing.

WATCH THE EXPERIMENT: Scan this QR code with your mobile device to see this experiment in action!

HOW DOES IT WORK?

You have created a "double pendulum" system where the two pendulums are connected by the same string, the pendulum strings are the same length and the weights have the same mass. Your careful measurements created two pendulums with the same **frequency**, or the number of back-and-forth swings there are in a second. Every time the first pendulum swings, the connecting string gives the second pendulum a small tug, making it swing as well. Since the second pendulum has the same frequency as the first, the tug occurs in a position that adds to the movement of the second pendulum.

The tugging of one pendulum on the other occurs because they swing slightly out of phase with each other. Think of a person pushing someone else on a swing as they are moving backward as opposed to forward—the push interferes with the swinger's momentum, and so they slow down rather than speed up. As soon as the second pendulum begins to swing, it starts pulling back on the first pendulum. These pulls are applied at the wrong place in the first pendulum's movement, so the effect is additive. The result is that the first pendulum slows down.

Eventually, the first pendulum is brought to rest when it has transferred all of its energy to the second pendulum. Now their roles are reversed: The first pendulum is motionless and all of the energy is now within the second pendulum. The process repeats itself with the two pendulums reversing roles until eventually all of the energy is removed from the system.

TAKE IT FURTHER

YOU CAN experiment with a friend, but this time, tell them that they can use the power of their mind to stop the first swinging weight: "Use the power of your mind to make the [object you used as a weight] slow down and stop...you did it!"

Once the second weight starts moving, quickly say, "Now move your concentration to the [other object] and make it slow down...more...more... and make it stop. Wow!"

DID YOU KNOW?

AROUND 1583, THE ITALIAN SCIENTIST GALILEO GALILEI OBSERVED A SWINGING LAMP IN A PISA CATHEDRAL AND REALIZED IT WAS MOVING AT A CONSTANT RATE—HE USED HIS PULSE RATE FOR COMPARISON. THIS INCIDENT INSPIRED HIM TO CONDUCT FURTHER RESEARCH ON THE TIMEKEEPING PROPERTIES OF PENDULUMS, BEGINNING IN 1602.

BED OF NAILS

⚠️ **SAFETY NOTE**
Have an adult help you with this experiment!

MATERIALS

2 Pieces of Wood (5 x 12 x ½ Inches)

2 Wooden Dowel Rods (9 Inches Long and ¾ Inch in Diameter)

Hammer

Nails

Ruler

Wood Glue

11-Inch Balloons

LET'S EXPERIMENT TO BUILD IT...

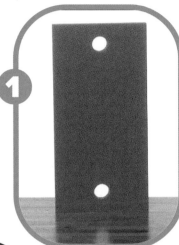

1 **DRILL** holes in the boards to accommodate the dowel rods.

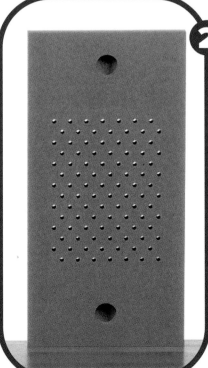

2 **THE** grid of nails on the bottom board has 7 rows and 14 columns. It's important to remember that there is nothing special about the size of this grid. The spacing of the nails is determined by the size of the nail head. Roofing nails have a large, flat head. It's important the nails are as close together as possible.

Have an adult pre-drill all of the holes using a drill bit that is slightly smaller than the nail. You want the nails to fit into the board snugly when you tap them in with a hammer.

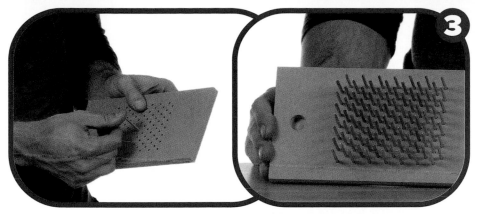

ASK an adult to help you tap all of the nails into the holes with a hammer.

GLUE the wooden dowel rods into the holes in the bottom board. These rods serve as guides to help hold the top board in place as you push down on the balloon.

TO CONDUCT THE EXPERIMENT...

BLOW UP one of the 11-inch balloons to a moderate size.

IF you have an extra nail, use it to prove to your audience that the nails are indeed sharp. Push the single nail into the balloon until it pops... which should be very easy to do.

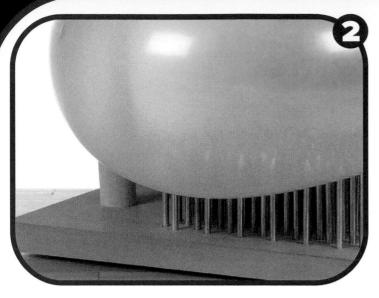

BLOW up another balloon and gently rest it on the bed of nails.

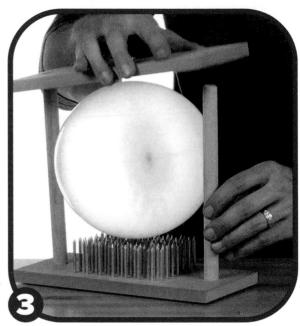

PLACE the top board over the dowel rods and gently rest the board on the balloon.

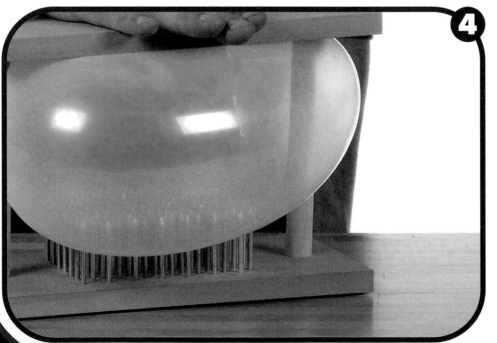

USE your hand to carefully push down on the top board to see how much pressure it takes to pop the balloon. To everyone's amazement, you can push down really hard without popping the balloon. Make sure to keep your hands clear of the nails!

INSTEAD of pushing down with your hand, you can stack books onto the top board. Keep adding books one at a time until the balloon pops.

HOW DOES IT WORK?

When you pushed the single nails into the balloon, you probably popped it immediately with very little pressure. The same thing would happen if you were to try to lay down on a single nail because all of that pressure is concentrated on a single point. The same is true for even five and 10 nails. The reason so little pressure is necessary to pop the balloon is because of surface area. All of the pressure on the balloon is being distributed to only one, five, or 10 points on the balloon, and this high concentration of pressure on very little area causes the nails to puncture the balloon.

When you increase the number of nails in the wooden base to 98 nails, you increase the number of points that the pressure is applied to. With these additional "pressure points," the force applied to the balloon is spread out across a large surface area of the balloon. That is why more pressure is necessary to pop the balloon.

Just like the balloon, when a performer at the circus lies on a bed of nails, their body is evenly distributed across the surface of the nails. The only real danger of being punctured by a nail is if the performer doesn't lie down or get up correctly and pressure points of the nails are concentrated on one area of the body. Now you know the circus secret!

TAKE IT FURTHER

YOUR LOCAL science museum just might have a bed of nails demonstration that is safe for you to try out. With your adult's permission, you'll start by laying down on a large sheet of plastic with thousands of little holes. When you push the button, thousands of nails push up and through the holes, lifting your body all at once! Surprisingly enough, it doesn't hurt because the weight of your body is being distributed across all of those nails.

DID YOU KNOW?

IT'S UNKNOWN **EXACTLY WHEN HUMANS BEGAN USING NAILS, BUT EVIDENCE OF NAILS USED BY ANCIENT EGYPTIANS DATES BACK TO AROUND 3400 B.C.**

INSANE SCIENCE

Take things up a notch with pyrotechnics, explosions and flying colors!

INCLUDES

BURNING MONEY

EXPLODING PAINT CANS

AWESOME AIR LAUNCHER

BURNING MONEY

⚠️

SAFETY NOTE
Have an adult help you
with this experiment! This
experiment utilizes fire, so it
should be conducted outside.

MATERIALS

70 Percent Rubbing Alcohol

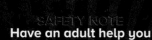
Tongs

Dollar Bill

Water

Lighter or Match

Safety Glasses

Fire Extinguisher (Just in Case)

Glass

LET'S EXPERIMENT

COMBINE 3 ounces (90 mL) of rubbing alcohol with 1 ounce (30 mL) of water. Stir the mixture thoroughly.

1

USING the tongs, dip the $20 bill into the mixture, making sure the bill gets completely soaked. Gently shake off any excess liquid.

MOVE the water-alcohol mixture to a safe place (away from the area where you are going to light the bill on fire).

**READ THIS STEP
BEFORE YOU DO IT:**
Using the tongs, hold the top
of the bill and have an adult
light the bottom of the bill with
a lighter. Observe.

3

THE bill will look
like it's burning,
but it shouldn't
burn. Do NOT
touch it!

RECORD how much time it takes for the flames to burn out.

WHEN the flame is completely extinguished, it's safe to touch the money. You'll find that the bill is even cool to the touch. How is that possible?

HOW DOES IT WORK?

You might've guessed that the money would actually burn if you dipped it into a pure alcohol solution. The secret, of course, is the addition of water to the mixture.

When the soaked bill comes into contact with the flame, the water evaporates and absorbs much of the heat energy that is generated upon ignition. After the water is heated to its **boiling point**, it's then vaporized by the heat of **combustion** from the burning alcohol, and the **evaporation** of the water keeps the temperature below the ignition point of paper, which is **451 degrees F or 233 degrees C.**

If you were to reduce the amount of water in the mixture, the paper money would likely char or even catch on fire.

As you can see in the photos, we used a $20 bill for this experiment, which depicts U.S. president Andrew Jackson. Twenty-dollar bills as we know them today have been in circulation since about 1861 and have featured portraits of other political figures including Abraham Lincoln, Alexander Hamilton and Grover Cleveland.

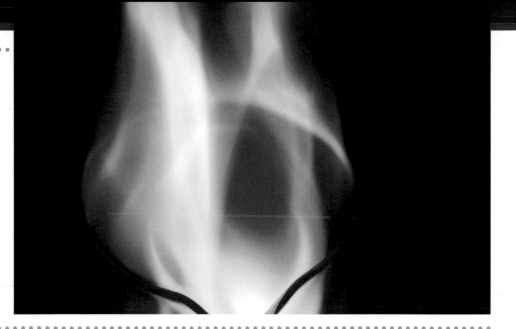

TAKE IT FURTHER

ALCOHOL BURNS with an almost invisible blue flame. One trick is to add a little table salt to the water-alcohol mixture to give the flame a yellowish color and make it more visible. You can also try to change the ratio of rubbing alcohol to water to see how it affects the way the bill burns, but you're likely to accidentally burn up your cash.

DID YOU KNOW?

FAHRENHEIT 451, A 1953 NOVEL BY RAY BRADBURY ABOUT BURNING BOOKS, IS SO NAMED DUE TO THE TEMPERATURE AT WHICH PAPER BURNS.

EXPLODING PAINT CANS

SAFETY NOTE

Have an adult help you with this experiment! This experiment is MESSY, so do it outside.

MATERIALS

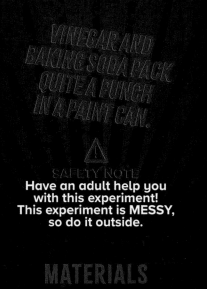

Baking Soda

Hammer

Large Bottle of Vinegar

Empty Gallon-Size Paint Can

Safety Glasses

Measuring Cup

Disposable Plastic Cup (Between 9 and 12 Ounces)

LET'S EXPERIMENT

GO OUTSIDE and find a flat surface away from anything you don't want covered in baking soda and vinegar.

IF YOU'VE never mixed vinegar and baking soda, try it! Combine 2 ounces of vinegar with 1 teaspoon of baking soda in a glass or a bowl to observe the incredible fizzing reaction that occurs. The combination of these two chemicals produces carbon dioxide, a gas that will provide the popping power you need to blow the paint can lid sky high.

1

MEASURE and pour 1 heaping cup of baking soda (about 250 grams) into the empty paint can.

2

FILL the disposable plastic cup with about 9 ounces of vinegar.

3

PUSH the baking soda to the side of the can to make room for the plastic cup to sit flat on the bottom. Carefully place the plastic cup into the can.

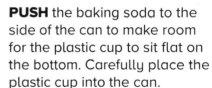

PUT on your safety glasses, then gently hammer the lid onto the can, making sure it's tight and being careful not to knock over the vinegar. Stand to the side of the can while hammering the lid in case the reaction starts prematurely.

If all goes well, the vinegar and baking soda will remain separated until you want the reaction to start.

4

5 **WHEN** you're ready, give the can a quick shake, just enough to mix the two chemicals. Quickly set the can down and move away!

OBSERVE.
The buildup of pressure from the bubbling carbon dioxide gas will be enough to make the lid pop off!

6

SAFETY NOTE
If the lid does NOT pop off...
It's possible that not enough carbon dioxide gas was generated to blow off the lid, but there still might be a buildup of pressure from the gas that needs to be released. If nothing happens after a few minutes, have an adult carefully approach the can and tip it so the lid is facing away from everyone. They can pry open the lid with a screwdriver to release the pressure. (If the lid was not completely hammered down, the carbon dioxide gas leaked out, in which case, try again.)

HOW DOES IT WORK?

The reaction that happens from mixing vinegar and baking soda is caused by the chemical reaction between the **acetic acid (CH_3COOH)** in vinegar and the **sodium bicarbonate ($NaHCO_3$)** in baking soda.

This reaction forms sodium acetate ($NaCH_3COO$), water (H_2O), and carbon dioxide (CO_2).

The chemical equation is as follows:

$$CH_3COOH + NaHCO_3 \rightarrow NaCH_3COO + H_2O + CO_2$$

The trick is to find the right amount of vinegar and baking soda that will produce more carbon dioxide gas than the container can hold so that the lid pops off...KABOOM!

As detailed in the Take It Further section, adding a few drops of soap produces lots of suds because small amounts of carbon dioxide gas get trapped in the soap. Neat!

TAKE IT FURTHER

TRY ANY one of these twists or variations to see what happens.
- Change the amount of vinegar or baking soda.
- Add a few drops of dish soap to the vinegar.
- Try the same reaction in a large zipper-lock bag rather than a paint can.
- Add a little bit of washable tempera paint for an amazing explosion of color.

DID YOU KNOW?

THE FIRST RESEALABLE TIN PAINT CAN WAS PATENTED BY SHERWIN-WILLIAMS IN 1877. BEFORE THAT TIME, LEFTOVER PAINT WAS SIMPLY DISCARDED. SAVE THE PAINT!

SUPER SODA DISPENSER

MATERIALS

Several 2-Liter Bottles of Diet Soda

6 Plastic Cups

PVC Pipes and Fittings

Mentos

Duct Tape

Drill

Toothpick

Ball Bearing (Optional)

Small Magnet (Optional)

LET'S EXPERIMENT

There's no one right way to build the soda dispenser, but this is our preferred setup.

Our design uses **six short pieces of ¾" PVC pipe, seven T connectors, six long pieces of ¾" PVC pipe and two PVC plugs**. Each pipe piece should fit snugly into the T connectors. You'll also need **one medium-length piece of ¾" PVC pipe** that will descend from the central T connector to the 2-liter bottle. (The piece of pipe we used is clear, but that's for demonstration purposes. You can use standard PVC instead.)

You should be able to find all of these items in the plumbing aisle of your local hardware store. Bring your bottle and a roll of Mentos to make sure the pieces you select are the right size for what you need.

Feel free to come up with your own variation based on the equipment you have handy.

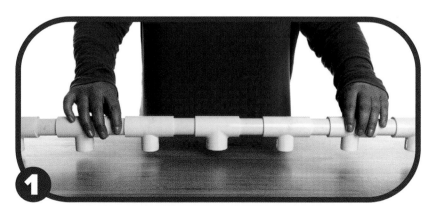

1

CONNECT the six short pieces and seven T connectors as shown. Add a plug to each end of the T connectors, otherwise you'll be bathing in soda.

INSERT the six long pieces into your dispenser as shown.

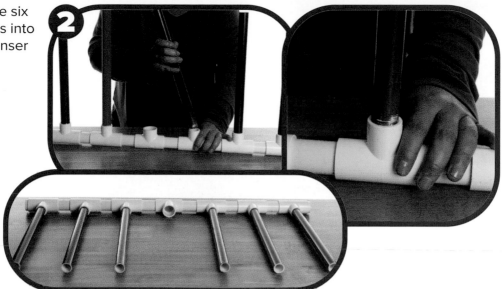

LOAD three to five Mentos into the medium-length piece of PVC pipe. We used a ball bearing and a strong magnet to keep the Mentos in place. You can also drill two holes at the bottom of the tube that are just big enough to hold a toothpick, then thread the toothpick through the tube, which will prevent the Mentos from falling into the soda.

NOTE: The red tube we used is a gadget called a Tornado Tube, which we'll use connect the medium-length piece of PVC to the 2-liter bottle. You can use duct tape to do the same job. Just be careful not to let your Mentos drop into the soda as you complete the next steps!

ONCE the Mentos are secured, fit the open end of the PVC pipe into the central T connector. If the fit isn't snug, use duct tape to make it airtight.

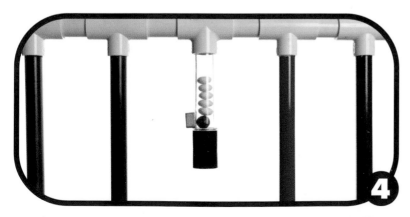

ATTACH the end of the diet soda bottle to the PVC holding the Mentos. Remember to use duct tape if you don't have a Tornado Tube. Once everything is secure, place each plastic cup beneath each long PVC pipe to catch the soda.

READ THIS STEP BEFORE YOU DO IT: If you're using the ball bearing/magnet setup, all you need to do is pull the magnet away from the pipe. The ball bearing will fall into the soda and the Mentos will follow. If you're using the toothpick method, simply pull the toothpick out of the tube. Either way, the resulting chemical reaction will drive the liquid up, through and down the pipes, filling each cup with a nice bubbly serving of soda!

HOW DOES IT WORK?

Soda is composed of sugar (or diet sweetener), flavoring, water and preservatives, and the thing that makes soda bubbly is invisible carbon dioxide (CO_2) gas, which is pumped into bottles at the factory using tons of pressure. Until you open the bottle and pour a glass of soda, the gas mostly stays suspended in the liquid and cannot expand to form more bubbles.

But if you shake the bottle and then open it, the gas is released from the protective hold of the water molecules and escapes, taking some of the soda along with it. How else can you cause the gas to escape? Try dropping something into a glass of soda and notice how bubbles immediately form on the surface of the object. For example, adding salt to soda causes it to foam up because thousands of little bubbles form on the surface of each grain of salt.

The surface of each Mentos candy is covered in thousands of tiny pits called nucleation sites, which are perfect places for CO_2 bubbles to form. As soon as the Mentos hit the soda, bubbles form all over the surface of the candy. Couple this with the fact that the Mentos candies are heavy and sink to the bottom of the bottle and you've got a double-whammy. When all this gas is released, the expanding CO_2 pushes all of the liquid up and out of the bottle in an incredible soda blast.

Why should you use diet soda? The short answer is diet soda simply works better than regular soda. Some people speculate the reason has something to do with the inclusion of artificial sweetener, but the verdict is still out.

DID YOU KNOW?

YOU CAN SEE A SIMILAR EFFECT WHEN A SCOOP OF ICE CREAM IS ADDED TO ROOT BEER TO CREATE A ROOT BEER FLOAT—THE FLOAT FOAMS OVER FOR ESSENTIALLY THE SAME REASON. THE SURFACE TENSION OF THE ROOT BEER IS LOWERED BY GUMS AND PROTEINS FROM THE MELTING ICE CREAM, AND THE CO_2 BUBBLES EXPAND AND RELEASE EASILY, CREATING A BEAUTIFUL (AND DELICIOUS) FOAM ON TOP.

FIRE TORNADO

⚠️

Have an adult help you with this experiment!

MATERIALS

Lazy Susan

Metal Screen (Similar to a Window Screen)

Wire or Staples

Lighter

Kitchen Sponge

Small Glass Dish

Lighter Fluid

Scissors

Small Square Plate

Fire Extinguisher (Just in Case)

Safety Glasses

Glass Dinner Plate (or Something Similar to Cover the Fire)

LET'S EXPERIMENT

NOTE: This experiment involves fire and MUST be conducted with an adult, outside, in an area with little to no wind.

IF you don't have a Lazy Susan, you can also look for an old record player at a thrift store, garage sale or flea market. With a little modification, you'll be able to transform the turntable into the spinning platform needed for your experiment.

1

EXAMINE the photos of the wire screen tube that follow. Find an adult to help you shape and hold it in place as you roll the screen into a cylinder that's a little smaller in diameter than the Lazy Susan. While constructing this tabletop version of the Fire Tornado, keep the height of the screen tube between 2½ and 3 feet tall. Anything taller might fall over while spinning.

FASTEN the ends of the cylinder using wire or staples. Rivets or wire can be used to secure the center section.

POSITION the wire cylinder in the middle of the Lazy Susan, then give it a gentle spin. You should be able to make the cylinder spin slowly without having to fasten it to the tray.
NOTE: You and an adult will need to be able to quickly remove the screen from the rotating tray and cover the fire with a plate to extinguish it.

SAFETY NOTE: If the screen cylinder is not positioned in the very middle of the tray, the cylinder will spin off-center and might fall over. The better you center the screen, the more even the spin will be, which will result in the best tornado possible.

PLACE the small glass dish in the middle of the Lazy Susan. It's best to find a small square of fire-resistant material (or a small plate or saucer) for the dish to sit on so as not to damage the Lazy Susan.

USING scissors, cut your sponge into several smaller pieces and place them in the dish. Pour lighter fluid on the pieces until they're completely soaked. There shouldn't be any liquid pooled up in the bottom of the dish, so make sure not to oversaturate the sponge pieces.

5

WEARING your safety glasses, have an adult light the sponges with a lighter. Leave the mesh screen off of the Lazy Susan for now and gently it. Observe.

NOTICE how the fire spins, but there's no tornado effect. Extinguish the fire by placing a plate on top.

6

REIGNITE the fire and place the wire screen cylinder back on the Lazy Susan. Gently spin it and observe as the fire twists into the shape of a tornado. The fire tornado will rise as the tray spins faster.

REMOVE the screen cylinder from the tray and extinguish the fire.

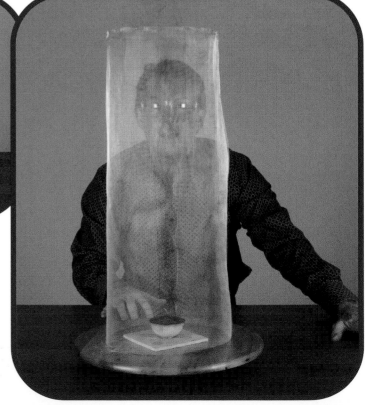

HOW DOES IT WORK?

Spinning the tray alone does not whip the fire into a twirling tornado, but when you center the fire in the middle of the rotating screen, you create the perfect fire tornado. It all starts with the heat from the flame that causes the surrounding molecules of air to rise. Couple this with the rotational motion of the screen and voilà: You have the perfect storm.

The rotating screen gives the air molecules angular momentum. The vertically rising hot air molecules collide with the rotating screen, and the angular momentum of the screen is transferred to the rapidly rising air molecules, giving them a "twist." Fresh air fuels the fire from the bottom, and the growing flames reach and twist into the shape of a tornado.

TAKE IT FURTHER

CREATE WIRE CYLINDERS using different types of metal screens: large mesh or small mesh constructed out of thin or thick wire. Each variation will produce a different effect. Don't be surprised if the thick wire, larger mesh screen doesn't work at all. Why do you think that is?

DID YOU KNOW?

FIREFIGHTERS SOMETIMES **BATTLE FIRE TORNADOES WHILE FIGHTING FOREST FIRES. THESE CAN TOWER 100 TO 200 FEET (OR 30 TO 50 METERS) TALL, AND SOME HAVE MEASURED HALF A MILE (OR MORE THAN A KILOMETER) IN HEIGHT. FIRE TORNADOES OCCUR WHEN WINDS WHIP THROUGH THE TREES AND COLLIDE WITH THE WARM UPDRAFT FROM THE WILDFIRE.**

CORNSTARCH QUICKSAND

MATERIALS

16-Ounce Box of Cornstarch

Large Mixing Bowl

Pitcher of Water

Cookie Sheet, Square Cake Pan or Something Similar

Spoon

Gallon-Size Zipper-Lock Bag

Newspaper or Plastic Drip Cloth (To Cover the Floor)

Toy Animal

LET'S EXPERIMENT

1

POUR one-quarter of the box of cornstarch (about 4 ounces) into the mixing bowl, then slowly add about a half cup of water and stir. If you don't mind getting messy, feel free to mix the cornstarch and water with your bare hands.

CONTINUE adding cornstarch and water in small amounts until you get a mixture that has the consistency of honey. (It may take a little work to get the consistency just right, but you will eventually end up mixing one box of cornstarch

2

with roughly 1 to 2 cups of water.) As a rule of thumb, you're looking for a mixture of roughly 10 parts cornstarch to one part water. Notice that the mixture gets thicker, or more viscous, as you add more cornstarch.

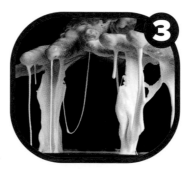

3

SINK your hand into the bowl of quicksand and notice its unusual consistency. Try moving your hand around slowly and then quickly. As it turns out, you can't move your hand around very fast—in fact, the faster you thrash around, the more solid the gooey mixture becomes. Sink your entire hand into the goo and try to grab the fluid and pull it up. That's the sensation of sinking in quicksand!

4

POUR the mixture onto the cookie sheet or cake pan and notice its unusual consistency. Stir it around with your finger, first slowly, then as fast as you can. Skim your finger across the top of the glop. What do you notice? You can even hold your hand flat over the top of the pan and slap the liquid glop as hard as you can. According to theory, the mixture should stay in the pan. If your cornstarch-water mixture splatters everywhere, however, you'll know to add more cornstarch. Finally, push your hand down into the liquid and quickly lift up. If the pan is light enough, it should stick to your hand.

WHEN you're finished, pour the mixture into a zipper-lock bag and toss it into the garbage.

TAKE IT FURTHER

TRY TO roll the fluid between your palms to make a ball. You'll find that by rolling with the right amount of speed, under the right amount of pressure, the ball will hold its shape. Once you stop rolling, however, it reverts back to liquid form. Try to see how big a ball you can create. Is there a certain point at which you can't roll the ball in a way that enables it to keep its shape? Why do you think that is?

HOW DOES IT WORK?

This cornstarch and water concoction is an example of a **suspension**: a mixture of two substances, one of which is finely divided and dispersed in the other. In this case, it's a solid dispersed in a liquid. When you slap the cornstarch quicksand, you force the long starch molecules closer together, and the impact of this force traps the water between the starch chains to form a semirigid structure. When the pressure is released, the cornstarch flows again. All fluids have a property known as **viscosity**—the measurable thickness or resistance to flow in a fluid. Honey and ketchup are liquids that have a high viscosity, whereas water has a low viscosity. According to Sir Isaac Newton, viscosity is a function of temperature; for example, if you heat honey, the viscosity is less than that of cold honey. The cornstarch-water mixture is an example of an **oobleck**, a **non-Newtonian fluid**, because its viscosity changes when stress or a force, rather than heat, is applied.

DID YOU KNOW?

QUICKSAND IS **FOUND AROUND RIVERBANKS, LAKES, BEACHES OR ANYWHERE AN UPRISING OF WATER OVERSATURATES AND AGITATES SANDY GROUND. THE REASON PEOPLE CANNOT DROWN IN QUICKSAND ALONE IS BECAUSE QUICKSAND IS DENSER THAN THE HUMAN BODY, MEANING IT WILL NOT COMPLETELY ENGULF SOMEONE TRAPPED IN IT. IT IS POSSIBLE, HOWEVER, THAT SOMEONE STUCK IN QUICKSAND—SAY, NEAR A BEACH— COULD DROWN IF THE TIDE ROLLED IN BEFORE THEY COULD BE RESCUED.**

AWESOME AIR LAUNCHER

⚠️
SAFETY NOTE
Have an adult help you with this experiment!

NOTE
This experiment is MESSY and should be performed outside!

MATERIALS

5-Gallon Bucket or Large Trash Can

Bungee Cord

Knife, Keyhole Saw or Drill with a Hole Saw Bit

Clear Plastic Shower Curtain or Thick Plastic Sheet

LET'S EXPERIMENT

1 **HAVE** an adult carefully cut a 2- to 3-inch diameter hole in the bottom center of the bucket.

STRETCH a piece of clear shower curtain or plastic sheet over the top of the bucket, then secure it in place using a bungee cord or large rubber band. This will act as the "membrane" across the top of the bucket.

2

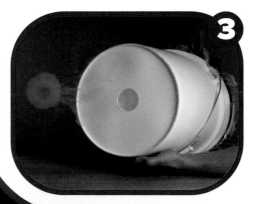

3 **LIGHTLY** hit the shower curtain with your hand or the end of a stick. An invisible blast of air shoots out of the hole.

NOTE: Smoke has been added to this step to help you see the effect of air shooting from the bucket.

Now try the larger version, which uses a plastic trash can in place of the smaller bucket!

CAREFULLY cut an 8-inch diameter hole in the bottom of the trash can.

STRETCH a piece of clear shower curtain or a plastic sheet over the top of the trash can and secure it in place using a bungee cord.

AIM the hole in the bottom of the trash can at a friend and smack the membrane. The blast of air is strong enough to startle an unsuspecting person.

TAKE IT FURTHER

HOW CAN you make the invisible blast of air visible? Try adding a little smoke. Believe it or not, the so-called blast of air is actually shaped like a ring, and just a little smoke will make the rings visible.

HOW TO MAKE A SMOKE RING LAUNCHER

FILL the bucket or trash can with a little theatrical smoke. Just position the hole in the trash can or bucket up against a smoke machine and give it a blast. Smoke machines (foggers) are commonly used in stage productions and are available at department stores around Halloween. You just need enough smoke to fill the container—a quick blast will do the trick.

AIM the hole in the bottom of the container up into the air and gently tap the shower curtain (a hard smack results in a fast blast of air that is difficult to see). The flying vortices are best seen against a dark background with light coming from either side. With a little practice, you can use the power of the smoke ring to knock a cup off of a fence or a chair from a distance of 20 to 30 feet!

FOURTH OF JULY SMOKE BOMB TWIST

PLACE a smoke bomb on a flat surface, then light it.

USE the hole in the bottom of the trash can to cover the smoke bomb and fill the can with smoke. Use caution, as hot debris can shoot up from the smoke bomb and burn tiny holes in the plastic membrane. The trash can is ready for you to tap the membrane and produce dozens of colorful smoke rings.

SAFETY NOTE: Never shoot smoke in the face of a person or animal! Aim the flying rings of smoke in the air and fire away.

HOW DOES IT WORK?

The proper name for the air cannon device is a **vortex generator**. The blast of air that shoots out of the cannon is actually a flat vortex of air, similar to rings of smoke blown by a cigar smoker (not that I endorse that!).

A vortex is generated because the air exiting the container at the center of the hole is traveling faster than the air exiting around the edge of the hole.

Bernoulli's Principle states that the faster a flow of air is moving, the lower its pressure. Since the air inside the vortex is moving faster than the outside air, the resulting inward pressure is the force that holds the smoke ring together. Eventually, air friction steals away all the energy stored in the vortex and the smoke ring drifts to a stop. Awesome!

This activity demonstrates the simple concept that air occupies space and that fast-moving air creates an area of low pressure. The flying smoke rings are an added bonus.

DID YOU KNOW?

BERNOULLI'S PRINCIPLE **DOESN'T JUST EXPLAIN HOW AIRPLANES CAN ACHIEVE LIFT. YOU'VE ALSO FELT BERNOULLI'S PRINCIPLE IN ACTION IF YOU'VE EVER STOOD NEAR THE EDGE OF A TRAIN PLATFORM AND FELT A SLIGHT PULL TOWARD THE TRACKS WHILE A TRAIN RUSHED PAST.**

BERNOULLI BLASTER

MATERIALS

Tall Glass

Drill

2 Straws (Preferably Bendy)

Water

PVC Pipe

Puffed Rice Cereal or Cheese Balls

Duct Tape

Shop Vacuum

Ping Pong Balls

Toothpick

Bucket

Leaf Blower

DWV PVC 2-Inch T Pipe

Safety Glasses

Assortment of PVC Fittings

2 Clear Plastic Fluorescent Tube Guards (48 Inches)

LET'S EXPERIMENT

BEFORE YOU GET STARTED...
This experiment has three different stages, each one bigger than the last. The first two are easy to execute. The final version is more difficult to build but a whole lot of fun.

1

STAGE ONE

FILL a glass almost to the top with water. Place one straw in the glass and position the other straw close to the top of the first straw. Bendy straws work best because you'll want to adjust the angle of the second straw.

The object is to blow air as hard as you can through the second straw and across the opening of the straw that's submerged in the water. The trick, however, is to get the second straw positioned so that as much air as possible flows across the opening of the first straw. Don't give up—you have to blow hard and adjust the angle of the straw until you see the water being drawn up the first straw. Eventually, it will shoot out of the straw and across the table. Tell your friends and family to stay clear!

STAGE TWO

DO it again, this time using something other than water. Grab a shop vacuum, make sure the hose is attached, then turn it to reverse. This will make the air flow out of the hose like a giant hair dryer.

PLACE a PVC pipe into a bucket filled with puffed rice cereal or cheese balls, then blow the fast-moving air from the shop vac across the top of the pipe as shown. You'll need to experiment with the angle to cause the cheese balls or puffed rice to fly up and out of the tube. Once you get it just right, watch out!

WHEN you're done blowing food everywhere, switch the shop vac back to normal and clean up!

STAGE THREE

VISIT the hardware store, taking your leaf blower with you. First, visit the lighting department and pick up two fluorescent tube guards. These clear plastic tubes measure 48 inches long and 1½ inches in diameter. They're designed to slide over fluorescent light bulbs and are just a hair wider than the diameter of a ping pong ball.

GO to the plumbing department. Ask an employee to help you find a DWV PVC 2-inch T pipe. (DWV stands for drain/waste/vent.) It's shaped like a "T."

GET creative and devise a way to attach the 2-inch T pipe to the spout of the leaf blower. This can usually be accomplished by mixing and matching different sizes and types of PVC. We attached a 2-inch piece of PVC pipe to the end of the leaf blower and then attached the T fitting to the pipe.

NEXT, you'll need to find a "reducer" fitting called a bushing to narrow the two other ends of the T pipe down to 1.25 inches. In our design, we used a bushing that goes from 2 Inches to 1.25 inches. The goal is to find a fitting that allows you to attach the fluorescent tube guard to the T pipe. Don't give up! Just keep experimenting with various fittings until you find one that works.

WITH the leaf blower turned on, drop a ping pong ball into the top opening of the tee fitting.

WHOOSH! The stream of air will draw the ball downward and shoot it out the other end.

ATTACH the tube guards to both tee pipe openings. Wrap the points of connection with duct tape if they're still too loose. Drop a ping pong ball into the opening of the "feeder" tube and watch it shoot down and out of the launch tube.

NOTE: Never point a leaf blower at another person! Doing so could cause serious injury.

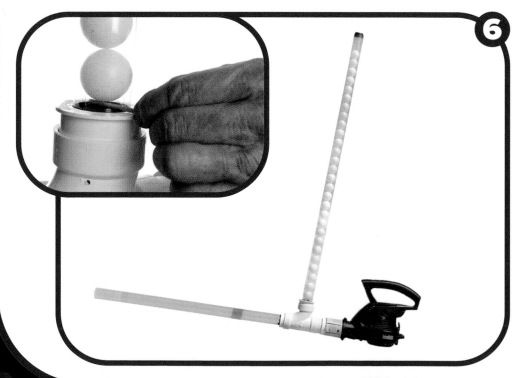

DRILL two holes at the base of the feeder tube just big enough to hold a toothpick or wooden cooking skewer. With the toothpick in place, fill the feeder tube with ping pong balls as shown. Fire up the leaf blower to allow the air to flow through the tube. Nothing happens until you pull the toothpick away...but watch out for the barrage of balls once you do!

HOW DOES IT WORK?

Bernoulli's Principle tells us that the faster air moves across an area, the more the pressure will decrease. So, as you blow across the opening of the vertical straw, there is a decrease in air pressure inside the straw. With a decrease of pressure inside the straw, the liquid is pushed up and out of the straw by the outside air pressure. Believe it or not, this is the same thing that happens when you suck on a soda straw. The "sucking" action actually reduces the air pressure inside the straw allowing the air pressure outside the straw to push on the soda in the glass, forcing it up and into your mouth.

Bernoulli's principle works for both liquids

and gases. The airstream from a typical leaf blower may range from 125 to over 200 miles per hour. The ping pong ball is very close to the diameter of the clear tube barrel, so the air is forced to push the ball down the tube. Since each ping pong ball is so light, the airflow can easily accelerate the ball to well over 100 miles per hour.

The feeder tube (the tube that holds all of the ping pong balls) uses a combination of gravity and atmospheric pressure to help feed those balls into the barrel chamber. If the tube is pointed toward the ground instead of straight up, the balls, bits of paper or small light objects can be forced up the tube somewhat like a vacuum cleaner.

DID YOU KNOW?

THIS IS HOW MANY PERFUME BOTTLES WORK: PUSHING DOWN ON THE PERFUME DISPENSER CAUSES A STREAM OF AIR TO SHOOT ACROSS THE TOP OF A TUBE THAT GOES DOWN INTO THE BOTTLE OF PERFUME. THE SAME METHOD IS USED IN SPRAY BOTTLES, WEED KILLER, FERTILIZER, PAINT SPRAYERS AND OTHER APPLICATIONS WHERE A LIQUID NEEDS TO BE TURNED INTO A FINE MIST.

EXPLODING PAINT CANS (THE JUMBO-SIZED VERSION)

TAKE THE EXPERIMENT FROM PG. 144 TO THE NEXT LEVEL!

⚠️

SAFETY NOTE

Have an adult help you with this experiment!

NOTE

This experiment is MESSY and should be performed outside!

MATERIALS

Baking Soda

Large Bottle of Vinegar

Gorilla Glue

Measuring Cup

9 Empty Gallon-Size Paint Cans

Hammer

Safety Glasses

Bottles of Tempera Paint

Duct Tape

Large Piece of Cardboard (or Painter's Canvas)

Plastic Tarp

9 Disposable Plastic Cups (Between 9 and 12 Ounces)

Steve demonstrated this large-scale experiment on *The Ellen DeGeneres Show*, where he and his demo team rigged a way to mount 120 paint cans on wooden planks that could be flipped over to trigger the explosion. Within seconds of triggering the reaction, the cans exploded with brightly colored paint flying everywhere—true science art.

There's a simple modification to the original experiment: Instead of shaking the can and running away, just turn the can upside down. When the chemicals mix and enough carbon dioxide is produced to break the seal, the can goes flying up into the air and the mixture of baking soda and vinegar shoots everywhere! If you add a squirt of tempera paint to the vinegar in the cup before you seal the lid, you get a very colorful explosion that is guaranteed to wow a crowd!

LET'S EXPERIMENT

COVER your outdoor workspace with a plastic tarp to help with cleanup. Assemble nine cans and place them in three rows of three (a 3 x 3 square grid). On the right, you'll see that Steve prepared 50 cans (!) and has also attached a rod to the bottom of each one, so that they could be mounted on wooden planks. Your setup will be simpler but just as fun (and messy).

1

MEASURE and pour one heaping cup of baking soda (about 250 grams) into each empty paint can. Fill each disposable plastic cup with about 9 ounces of vinegar (about 270 mL)and a squirt of tempera paint. Push the baking soda to the side of the can to make room for each plastic cup to sit flat on the bottom of each can before carefully adding each cup of vinegar.

WEARING your safety glasses, gently hammer the lid on each can tightly, making sure it's tight and being careful not to knock over the vinegar. Stand to the side of the can while you hammer the lid in case the reaction starts prematurely.

Add Gorilla Glue, loops of duct tape or another strong adhesive to the tops of your paint cans. Place a piece of plywood or a blank painter's canvas on top of the cans and allow the adhesive to dry.

WHEN you're ready, have a friend and an adult help you carefully lift then quickly flip over the cardboard so that the cans are upside down, then run away! Enjoy the show.

HOW DOES IT WORK?

For more info on why this activity works, turn to pg. 147!

DID YOU KNOW?

TEMPERA PAINT **IS LONG-LASTING AND ITS COLORS DON'T DARKEN OR FADE MUCH OVER TIME, WHICH EXPLAINS WHY SO MANY MEDIEVAL PAINTINGS CREATED WITH TEMPERA PAINT ARE STILL ENJOYED IN MUSEUMS TODAY, INCLUDING SANDRO BOTTICELLI'S MASTERPIECE "THE BIRTH OF VENUS" (c. 1485). ONCE MADE WITH EGG YOLKS, TEMPERA PAINTS FELL OUT OF POPULARITY DURING THE RENAISSANCE WITH THE ADVENT OF OIL PAINTING AROUND 1500.**

GLOSSARY

ACETIC ACID
A clear, colorless, strong-smelling liquid and chemical compound that's the main ingredient in vinegar (aside from water).

ACOUSTICS
The science and study of sound waves and their physical properties.

ADHESION
The attraction of like molecules to molecules of a different type.

AMPLITUDE
A way to measure a sound or light wave. Amplitude describes the height of a wave on a graph.

ASPARTAME
A white, low-calorie, artificial sweetener that is 200 times sweeter than sugar. Commonly used as a sugar substitute.

ATMOSPHERIC PRESSURE
The force exerted by air.

ATOMS
The smallest units of ordinary matter that make up a chemical element.

BERNOULLI'S PRINCIPLE
The speed of a fluid (a gas or liquid) is inversely related to the pressure of a fluid. As the speed of a fluid increases, its pressure decreases, and vice versa.

BOILING POINT
The temperature at which a liquid boils. Water's boiling point is 212 degrees F (100 degrees C).

BOYLE'S LAW
A gas's pressure tends to decrease as the volume of its container increases and vice versa.

BUOYANCY
The upward force on an object created by a surrounding gas or liquid.

CARBON DIOXIDE
A colorless, odorless gas composed of carbon and oxygen.

CATALYST
A substance that causes or speeds up a chemical reaction yet remains unchanged.

CENTRIPETAL FORCE
A force that pushes an object along a circular path.

COHESION
The attraction of like molecules to one another.

COMBUSTION
A chemical reaction by which a fuel source and an oxidant combine to produce energy in the form of light and heat.

THE LAW OF CONSERVATION OF ENERGY
Energy can neither be created nor destroyed;

it can only change from one form to another.

CONVECTION
In terms of heat transfer, a movement in a liquid or gas in which warmer parts rise and cooler parts fall.

CREVASSE
A deep crack commonly found in glaciers that results from movement in the mass of ice.

DENSITY
A measure of how compact a substance is. Density equals mass divided by volume.

DISSOLVE
To become incorporated in liquid, forming a solution.

DRAG
A force caused by friction that slows a moving object. One of the four forces of flight.

ELASTOMER
A natural or synthetic polymer that possesses rubber-like, elastic properties.

ENDOTHERMIC REACTION
A chemical reaction in which energy is absorbed, resulting in a cooling (as opposed to warming) effect.

EVAPORATION
The process by which liquid molecules transform into air molecules.

EXOTHERMIC REACTION
A chemical reaction in which energy is released as heat, generating warmth.

FORCE
An influence that changes the motion of a body.

FREEZING POINT
The temperature at which a liquid becomes a solid. Water freezes at 32 degrees F (0 degrees C).

FREQUENCY
The number of times an event repeats in a given unit of time.

FRICTION
The resistance that occurs when one object moves over another.

FULCRUM
The pivot point on a lever.

GAS
A substance in a state that has no fixed shape or volume and will expand to fill whatever container it is in.

GRAVITY
The force that attracts everything to the center of the Earth, or any other body with mass.

HYDROGEN PEROXIDE
A colorless, reactive liquid commonly used in a diluted form as an antiseptic or as a bleaching agent.

HYDROPHILIC
Tending to mix with or dissolve in water.

HYDROPHOBIC
Tending to repel water.

INERTIA
The tendency of an object to either stay at rest or remain in motion.

GLOSSARY

KINETIC ENERGY
The energy of motion; potential energy is converted into kinetic energy as it is used.

LIFT
An upward force caused by differences in air pressure. One of the four forces of flight.

LIQUID
A substance that flows freely but has constant volume.

MASS
A measure of the amount of matter in an object.

MEMBRANE
A thin layer of cells or tissue that acts as a boundary within an organism.

MISDIRECTION
The process by which you shift someone's focus to something as a means of distraction, often while performing a magic trick.

MOLECULE
The smallest unit of a chemical compound that can be part of a chemical reaction.

MOMENTUM
The strength or force of an object in motion.

MONOMER
An atom or small molecule that bonds with like atoms or molecules, forming a chain called a polymer.

NEWTON'S FIRST LAW OF MOTION
Objects at rest tend to stay at rest and objects in motion tend to stay in motion unless acted on by an outside force.

NEWTON'S SECOND LAW OF MOTION
An object's acceleration depends on two variables: its mass and the force that is exerted on it.

NEWTON'S THIRD LAW OF MOTION
Every action has an equal and opposite reaction.

NON-NEWTONIAN FLUID
A substance that behaves like a liquid or a solid depending on whether or not it is subjected to force.

OOBLECK
A non-Newtonian fluid made of cornstarch and water.

OPTICAL ILLUSION
An image designed to trick your eyes into seeing something different than what is actually there.

PASCAL'S LAW
When pressure is applied to a contained fluid, the force disperses throughout the fluid in all directions in equal measure.

PENDULUM
A free-swinging weight suspended by a pivot originally used for timekeeping.

POLYMER
A chain of like molecules known as monomers.

POTENTIAL ENERGY
The stored energy an object has because of its position or state.

PRESSURE
A continuous force exerted on an object.

REACTION
A chemical process where two or more substances change one another into different substances.

SODIUM BICARBONATE
A white, crystalline, solid chemical compound commonly known as baking soda and frequently used as an antacid.

SODIUM IODIDE
A white or colorless water soluble chemical compound—a crystalline salt—that is commonly used as a nutritional supplement.

SOLID
A substance with a constant shape and volume.

SOLUBLE
Able to be dissolved in water. Something dissolved in water is called a solute.

SOLVENT
The liquid in which a solute is being dissolved.

SUBLIMATION
The process by which a solid transforms into a gas without first becoming a liquid.

SURFACE TENSION
A force in the surface layer of a liquid that causes it to act like an elastic sheet. This is caused by cohesion.

SUSPENSION
A heterogeneous (or compound) mixture in which small particles of a solid are suspended in a liquid but do not dissolve.

TEMPERATURE
A degree of heat or cold that can be measured with a thermometer.

THERMOMETER
A tool used for measuring temperature.

THRUST
The force that propels an object (like an aircraft) forward. One of the four forces of flight.

VISCOSITY
In reference to a fluid, the state of being sticky or glutinous—the thickness of fluid.

VOLUME
The amount of space taken up by an object.

VORTEX
A spinning, rotating column of fluid aligned along a straight or curved axis.

WEIGHT
The force exerted by gravity on an object. One of the four forces of flight.

STEVE SPANGLER

Since the early 1990s, Steve Spangler has been on a mission to get kids and adults alike excited about all things science. From his humble beginnings as a science teacher in Colorado to rocketing to viral internet fame in 2005 with his Mentos Diet Coke Experiment video on YouTube, in which he added Mentos candies to a bottle of diet soda to create a massive geyser, Spangler has become a household name. This is in part due to his frequent appearances as a beloved guest on *The Ellen DeGeneres Show*, with a whopping 27 visits in total!

Whether he's recording and uploading educational, exciting and explosion-filled content to social media platforms like Facebook, YouTube and Instagram or serving as the host of his television series *DIY Sci*, in which he teaches viewers how to create incredible at-home experiments all while using items found around the house, Spangler aims to reach his viewers by kindling a lifelong love of learning about the forces at work in our universe. Lovingly dubbed "America's Science Teacher" by Ellen DeGeneres, the Emmy Award-winning educator has racked up several stellar accolades: He holds a Guinness World Record for conducting the world's largest physics lesson in 2009, and he was inducted into the National Speaker Hall of Fame in 2010. When he isn't demonstrating awesome science experiments or engaging with the next generation of leaders as a STEM keynote speaker, Spangler is also a bestselling author whose credits include *Smithsonian 10-Minute Science Experiments*, *Naked Eggs and Flying Potatoes*, *Fire Bubbles and Exploding Toothpaste* and *Steve Spangler's Super-Cool Science Experiments for Kids*.

To learn more, visit *stevespangler.com*.

Media Lab Books
For inquiries, call 646-449-8614

Copyright 2022 Topix Media Lab

Published by Topix Media Lab
14 Wall Street, Suite 3C
New York, NY 10005

Printed in Korea

ISBN-13: 978-1-948174-94-7
ISBN-10: 1-948174-94-4

CEO Tony Romando

Vice President & Publisher Phil Sexton
Senior Vice President of Sales & New Markets Tom Mifsud
Vice President of Retail Sales & Logistics Linda Greenblatt
Chief Financial Officer Vandana Patel
Manufacturing Director Nancy Puskuldjian
Financial Analyst Matthew Quinn
Digital Marketing & Strategy Manager Elyse Gregov

Chief Content Officer Jeff Ashworth
Director of Editorial Operations Courtney Kerrigan
Creative Director Susan Dazzo
Photo Director Dave Weiss
Executive Editor Tim Baker

Content Editor Juliana Sharaf
Content Designer Mikio Sakai
Senior Editor Trevor Courneen
Assistant Managing Editor Tara Sherman
Designer Glen Karpowich
Copy Editor & Fact Checker Madeline Raynor
Junior Designer Alyssa Bredin Quirós
Assistant Photo Editor Jenna Addesso

All Steve Spangler Portraits and Step-by-Step Photos: Steve Spangler, Inc.
Step-by-Step Photography by Bryan Higgins

Photo Credits: 4 shironosov/iStock; 12 Jon Feingersh Photography Inc/Getty Images; 15 FatCamera/Getty Images; 16 Jamie Grill Photography/Getty Images; 39 Henry Burroughs/AP Images; 45 Alessandro0770/Alamy; 54 Courtney Hale/Getty Images; 99 Jacques Boyer/Roger Viollet via Getty Images; 102 Richard Hutchings/Getty Images; 138 Portra/Getty Images. Additional Photos and Art Elements: Shutterstock

© 2022 Topix Media

The experiments presented herein were originally featured on Steve Spangler's Sick Science! YouTube channel.

PA-E22-1